ISBN: 0-944094-43-0

Published by:
ST Books
ST Media Group International Inc.
407 Gilbert Avenue
Cincinnati, Ohio 45202
Tel. 513-421-2050
Fax 513-421-6110
E-mail: books@stmediagroup.com
www.stmediagroup.com

Distributed to the book and art trade by:
HarperCollins International
10 East 53rd Street
New York, NY 10022-5229

Book design by Kim Pegram, Art Director, VM+SD
Book compiled by Mackenzie Cohen and Alicia Hanson, Assistant Editors, VM+SD
Book edited by Matthew Hall, Managing Editor, VM+SD

Printed in China
10 9 8 7 6 5 4 3 2 1

Table of Contents

inventYOURSELF

Apparel

Displaying clothes has never been more exciting and challenging. With an increasingly diverse range of fixtures and forms, apparel retailers have discovered presentations that work well for one clothier many not transfer so successfully to another. For instance, while sleek and clean may be the right retail potion for Kenneth Cole, Hot Topic targets teen girls with a flashy merchandising concept that even boasts industrial insulating material like that found in dance clubs.

But for all successful apparel retailers, effective display relies on a combination of elements: lighting, mannequins/forms, clear and interesting signage, interactive and modular fixtures and a complementary materials palette from the floor up. All these parts must fit together to produce a visually pleasing design that will translate to constant and repeat customer traffic.

Here we show a diverse range of in-store apparel presentations. Marshall Field's "Les Shoes" presentation, for instance, conveyed a whimsical Parisian theme with a colorful wall mural that matched illustrations and mannequins in its window display. Meanwhile, Seibu Department Store used larger-than-life swirls and abstract feminine shapes to suggest movement in its "Summer 2000" presentations.

Hugo Boss

NEW YORK

The four-level, 22,000-square-foot Hugo Boss flagship store, with its wide-open four-story atrium and eye-popping wall art, is easily visible from the street. At street level, where high-fashion menswear is showcased, a nine-panel flat video wall divides this area from the Boss Woman boutique. Fold-down aluminum panels allow for an ever-changing presentation of shoes and accessories. The second floor offers casual clothing arranged in vivid color groupings on tiered oak tables with stainless-steel supports. Flat video panels divide and define these merchandise areas. The various floors are accessed by the seen-and-be-seen limestone staircase flanking the art wall.

Client Design Team
Hugo Boss America, New York – Marty Staff, ceo; Randy Yaw, visual manager; Design Pummer, Munich; Plan 2 Plus, Munich; Studio Invernizze, Milan

Architect of Record
The Phillips Group, New York – Steven Segure, project manager; Doris Almaza, project architect; Melissa Baker, job captain; Alec Zaballero, design liason; Alexander Yanno, project designer

Outside Consultants
Light Options, New York, JKLD, New York (lighting); Goldman Copeland, New York (MED); Severund, New York (structural)

Bang & Olufsen, Jutland, Denmark, Muzak, Seattle, Progressive IMG, New York (audio/visual); Hugo Boss Germany, Metzingen, Germany (fixturing, furniture); Ex Inc., New York (flooring); Erco Lighting, Edison, N.J. (general lighting); RSA Lighting, Chatsworth, Calif. (atrium lighting)

Photography
Richard Cadan, New York

visual merchandising 3 |

Nautica

NEW YORK

The Nautica flagship in Rockefeller Plaza combines former bank and movie theater spaces into a location that accommodates all its branded merchandise under one roof. Among the elements in the 12,000-square-foot store, off-white squares of a terrazzo look-alike cover much of the floor, interspersed with areas of bleached white oak and tobacco-leaf carpeting. Overhead, banks of authentic-looking "stage lights" suggest the steel skeleton of a ship's innards. A graceful, floating staircase with walnut treads ascends to the mezzanine, where vintage accent pieces like the antique fresnel light from a Maine lighthouse add interest and a sense of history.

Client Team
Nautica Intl., New York — David Chu, vice chairman and ceo; Joseph Lembo, vp, Nautica Creative and Store Design; Helen Windle, visual designer, Nautica Creative and Store Design

Design Team
Tsao + McKown Architects, New York — Calvin Tsao, AIA, principal; Elvis Wells, Adam Rolston, senior project managers; Bill Bonick, Maria Ibanez, Paul Lee, designers

Architect of Record
The Phillips Group, New York — John Szubski, Bill Wichart, George Rosa, Ronald Alalouf

General Contractor
Lehr Construction, New York

Suppliers
ECI Communications, S. Plainfield, N.J. (audio/visual); Techno Acoustics, Stamford, Conn. (ceilings); Randolph & Hein, New York, Bergamo, New York (fabrics); idX, Clayton, Mo. (fixturing fabrication); Lanzilotta, Brooklyn, N.Y., Durateck, Westchester County, N.Y. (flooring); Jean Brown, London, Wyeth, New York, Dansk Mobil Kunst, Copenhagen, Denmark (furniture); Seven Worldwide, Carlstadt, N.J. (graphics); Isometrix, London, AMA Engineers, New York, JDC Lighting, New York, Lutron, Coopersburg, Pa. (lighting); Adel Rootstein, New York and London, Bonaveri through George Dell, New York (mannequins); Guinevere, London, Wyeth, New York, Fisher Scientific, Hampton, N.H., D&A Binder, London, Furniture Co., New York (props and decoratives); Midtown Neon Sign Corp., New York (signage); Mary Bright Inc., New York (curtain fabrication)

Photography
Andrew Bordwin, New York

Chroma

MIAMI BEACH, FLA.

Bonnie Engelstein, owner of the Chroma women's boutique, asked BAMdesign (New York) to render the space as a gallery that would change with current fashion trends and also exhibit local artists. A floating ceiling was constructed to scale the vertical height and conceal the mechanical systems and lighting. Set within the floating ceiling is a perimeter lighting track that suspends the illuminated furniture displays and allows the store to change with the collections or transform for events such as fashion shows and art openings.

Client
Chroma – Bonnie Engelstein, owner

Design Team
BAMdesign, New York – Lisa Monteleone, project manager; Marco Bonelli

General Contractor
RCC Construction, Delray Beach, Fla. – Rick Rhodes, project manager

Architect
William Lane Architects, Miami Beach, Fla. – William Lane, project manager

Lighting Consultant
Muir Reality, New York – Ross Muir, project manager

Outside Design Consultants
Butter Graphics, Houston

Suppliers
Integrity Woodworks, Scott, La. (millwork); Castillio Fine Arts Upholstery, Hollywood, Fla. (furniture upholstery); IFORM, Malmo, Sweden (lounge chairs)

Photography
Ross Muir, New York

Aritzia

CALGARY, ALB.

When the Canadian clothing store chain Aritzia needed a prototype look for mall settings, the retailer started with its Calgary, Alb., store. Intended to appeal to 16- to 30-year-old women, the store features a white, minimalist architecture, with circular/square motifs of the 60s and 70s. Large, abstracted shapes dominate the space, including three oversized Plexiglas® lighting fixtures laminated in blonde-wood veneer that loom over the wooden display tables. At the back wall, an Australian walnut display fixture composed of stacked cylinders holds merchandise in square-shaped niches.

Client
  Aritzia, Vancouver – Brian Hill, owner

Design Team
  McKinley Dang Burkart Design Group, Calgary, Alb. – Mark Burkart, Walker McKinley and Nam Dang, partners/designers

Suppliers
  Acoustical Solutions, Richmond, Va. (flooring, ceiling); Lo Gullo, Calgary, Alb. (fixturing); McKinley Dang Burkart Design Group, Calgary, Alb. (furniture, graphics); Concepts in Wood, Calgary, Alb. (lighting fixtures); Topmade Signage, Calgary, Alb. (signage)

Photography
  Robert Lemermeyer, Calgary, Alb.

Caban

TORONTO

Caban's products are organized around themes. In the Outdoor Zone, an antique kayak is suspended from a dropped ceiling panel; outdoor-wear and a globe are presented on oak tables beside an oatmeal-colored recliner. The Bath Zone offers towels and toiletries on above-lit aluminum shelving, while the Spa Zone merchandise is featured on illuminated resin shelving. Downstairs, wet-looking topaz vinyl club chairs stand out on the dark jatoba wood floor. A bar and glassware suggest the chic of an urban apartment.

Client
    Club Monaco Inc., Toronto

Design Team
    burdifilek, Toronto – Diego Burdi, design director; Paul Filek, managing partner; Tom Yip, senior designer/project leader; Cathy Knott and Mariko Nakagawa, designers

Outside Design Consultants
    Maystar General Contractors, Concord, Ont. (general contractor); LKM Consulting Engineers, Toronto (engineers)

Suppliers
    Pancor Industries, Mississauga, Ont. (millwork); CB Metal, Toronto (metal work); Gem Campbell, Toronto (stone work); Industry Drywall, Toronto (ceiling, drywall); Antique Wood Flooring, Oakville, Ont. (wood flooring); Sullivan Source, Toronto (carpeting); TPL Marketing, Concord, Ont. (lighting); Saturn 18, Downsview, Ont. (audio/video); Formica, Cincinnati (laminates); Pittsburgh Paints, Pittsburgh (paint); Ginger's, Toronto (plumbing fixtures); Mayport Hardware, Toronto (hardware); Fireplace 2000, Toronto (fireplaces); Tasco, Toronto (kitchen appliances); Sunset Neon, Burlington, Ont. (signage/graphics)

Photography
    Evan Dion, Toronto

Marshall field's

CHICAGO

For the opening windows of the new shoe department at Marshall Field's State Street store, designer Chesley McClaren created a series of playful, stylish, faux-French illustrations. The 11 three-dimensional windows featured funny vignettes composed of mannequins, props and paint, the collection acting as a teaser several weeks before the department actually opened. Individual, colorfully painted shoes resided in smaller windows, while larger displays featured phrases like, "Shop til you drop!" and "Les Shoes pour Tous!" ("Shoes for all!")

Client Design Team
  Marshall Field's, Chicago/The Department Store Div. of Target Corp., Minneapolis — Donna Milano Johnson, window display manager; Jamie Becker, creative director of visual marketing; Amy Meadows, visual marketing manager

Outside Consultant
  Chesley McClaren, New York (illustrations)

Supplier
  Kinchromize, Chicago (backdrops, props)

Photography
  Susan Kezon, Chicago

Tobu Department Store

TOKYO

Inspired by the art of Robert Irwin, these Tobu Department Store windows in Tokyo used theatrical scrim to create a "soft spring haze." Mannequins were placed among the scrim panels, creating differing levels of obscurity and a sense of depth. Some of the windows' back walls were painted to create gradations of color projected on the scrim.

Client Team
Tobu Department Store, Tokyo

Design Team
Otsu Design, New York – Motonobu Otsu, art director and designer

Suppliers
Nomura Duo East, Tokyo (props)

Photography
Courtesy of Tobu Department Store, Tokyo

Kenneth Cole

NEW YORK

The 17,500-square-foot Kenneth Cole flagship in Rockefeller Center expresses the retailer's attitude of chic, urban energy in a clean, edgy setting. A "bridge" carries shoppers across an open stairwell, conserving selling space on the second level, where women's clothing is merchandised. Downstairs, the men's area is punctuated by computer kiosks that allow access to the Kenneth Cole web site. A neon-backlit frosted-glass display showcases men's shoes. Perhaps most dramatic is the 30-foot silk-and-polyester scrim curtain that hangs in the center of the stairwell.

Client Design
Kenneth Cole Productions Inc., New York

Concept Design
Studio Gaia, New York

Architect of Record
The Phillips Group, New York

Construction Manager
Lehr Construction, New York

Outside Design Consultants
Isometrix, London (lighting); TR Technologies, New York (audio/visual); Office of James Ruderman, New York (structural engineer); Robert Derector Associates, New York (mechanical and electrical engineer)

Suppliers
A-V Services, Fairfield, N.J. (audio/visual); TwentyFour•Seven Marketing Bloc Inc., Portland, Ore. (fabrics, fixturing, furniture); Light Options, New York (lighting)

Photography
Mark Ballogg, Steinkamp/Ballogg, Chicago

Liz Claiborne

LONDON

Taking a classic American brand to Europe involved making a two-floor, 3000-square-foot space resemble a tasteful home, full of innovative surfacing materials. Painted blue walls and blue laminate fixture panels define the ground-floor casual collection. A coffered ceiling with crown moulding marks the career collections area. Colored glass mosaic tiles behind the cashwrap brighten the store, while backlit aluminum-framed windows at the staircase draw customers to the atrium-like mezzanine level.

Design Team
    MOVK, New York – Mark Oller and Victoria Kirk, principals; Robert Nassar and Ricardo Marquez, design team

Outside Consultants
    Tienda Ltd., Gratham, England (architect of record/plumbing engineer); Rodgers, Clark Lander Ltd., Leicester, England (structural engineer); Cold Control Services Ltd., Alton, Hants, England (mechanical engineer); Dudley Bower Services Ltd., Grantham, England (electrical engineer)

Suppliers
    Harbinger, Atlanta (carpet); Bendheim Architectural Glass, New York (custom glass); Modular & Reggiani, London (display lighting); Angela Brown, New York (fabrics); Architectural Systems, New York (flooring); Peerless, London (metalwork); Artexture Plus, Toronto (textured wood); Bruno Triplet, London (upholstery)

Photography
    Andrew Lang, London

Carson Pirie Scott

SCHAUMBURG, ILL.

Renovating the space of the former Montgomery Ward store and abandoned movie theater was quite a challenge for designers. Because of the lone entrance, Carson's created two-sided merchandise presentations with mannequins and fixtures to play both outside to passersby, and inside to shoppers traversing the ring-road aisle through the store. Drywall ceiling drops follow the aisle, containing light coves that both reinforce the traffic patterns and keep the store bright. An open escalator well in the center of the store ensures that customers notice the second floor option. Seven-foot-high glass mobile walls provide vertical fixturing, flexible merchandising and departmental dividers.

Client Team
Saks Inc., Birmingham, Ala. – Ken Poston, vp, store planning; Jim Mitchell, director, planning and design; Rick Schlenther, vp, visual merchandising; Don Bruce, construction

Design Team
Johnson Design Group, Park Ridge, Ill. – Mark Johnson, principal; Paul Benes, project manager; Anna Gniewek, documentation

Suppliers
Armstrong World Industries, Lancaster, Pa. (ceilings); Mason Corp., St. Charles, Ill., MEI, Atlanta, Vira Mfg., Perth Amboy, N.J. (fixturing); Innovative Marble & Tile, Hauppauge, N.Y., Shaw Carpet, Dalton, Ga., Mannington Commercial Carpet, Calhoun, Ga. (flooring); Loewenstein Inc., Pompano Beach, Fla. (furniture); Lithonia Lighting, Conyers, Ga. (lighting); Pucci, New York, Silvestri California, Los Angeles, seven continents, Toronto (mannequins/forms); Silvestri California, Los Angeles, Look, New York, Elevations Inc., S. San Francisco, Calif. (props/decoratives); The Sign Centre, Chicago (signage); J.M. Lynne Wallcovering, Ronkonkoma, N.Y. (wallcoverings)

Photography
John Shelves, Summit Studio, Roselle, Ill.

Lillie Rubin

SAN ANTONIO

Lillie Rubin, the 50-year-old specialty clothing store chain, tapped Michael Malone Architects (Dallas) to conceive a fresh look that would attract new, younger customers without alienating the retailer's core, albeit aging, clientele. The bright, open, 2100-square-foot prototype features a cream and black palette that provides a luxurious backdrop to the clothing displayed along walls, in flexible bins, on hang bars and face-outs. Black and stainless-steel floor fixtures spotlight dresses. And the cashwrap, which doubles as a jewelry and fragrance display, takes the shape of a grand piano, also echoed in the ceiling overhead.

Client
Caché/Lillie Ruben, New York – Clifford Gray, vp, store design and construction

Architect
Michael Malone Architects Inc., Dallas – Michael Malone, principal-in-charge; Rob Romero, project manager; Talmadge Smith, project architect

General Contractor
Frandy Inc., Hackettstown, N.J.

Suppliers
Vision Woodworking, Fridley, Minn. (fixturing); GranitiFiandre, Ithaca, Ill. (flooring); Lightolier, Fall River, Mass. (lighting); Granata Sign, Stamford, Conn. (signage)

Photography
Jud Haggard Photography, Bellaire, Texas

Alberta Ferretti

TOKYO

When luxury fashion retailer Alberta Ferretti decided to open her first stand-alone store in Tokyo, designers at David Ling Architect (New York) conceptualized a fusion of layering, translucency, texture and craft that mimics the premier product. The 2000-square-foot location features Portuguese limestone flooring and hand-burnished mother-of-pearl-colored walls that lend a warm feel to the space. Massive lightboxes on both floors in the store's rear provide most of the illumination. A cone-shaped column made from ebonized American walnut links both floors, creating a dramatic focal point. The stairs feature steel beams clad in stone that appear to float with an all-glass railing.

Client Team
Alberta Ferretti, Emigla-Romagna, Italy – Massimo Ferretti, president; Alberta Ferretti, vp; Imamura, Sann Freres; Nakano, Mitsui & Co.

Design Team
David Ling Architect, New York – David Ling, principal-in-charge; Tina Jokisch, Yuri Premerlani, assistants

Outside Consultants
Garde U.S.P. Co. Ltd., Tokyo (ceilings, signage, wallcoverings, fixturing, furniture); Bose Japan, Tokyo (audio/video); Sangetsu Co. Ltd., Tokyo (fabrics); David Ling Architect, New York (fixturing/furniture design); Advan Co. Ltd., Tokyo (Portuguese limestone flooring); AEFFE S.P.A., Rimini, Italy (mannequins/forms)

Suppliers
David Ling Architect, New York (tables); Brown Grotta Gallery, Wilton, Ct. (art pieces); Herman Miller, Zeeland, Mich. (chairs)

Photography
Nacasa & Partners, Tokyo

The Limited

COLUMBUS, OHIO

The idea was to create a shopping experience that would establish The Limited as an authority on style for the young, professional American woman. The prototype store revolves around a three-room concept, in which different product stories are told. Right inside the entrance, a large platform with eight mannequins and several looks immediately grabs the customer's attention. A puck wall system, showcasing approximately 75 interrelated separates, helps the shopper visualize different wardrobe ideas. The contrast between the creamy lacquer walls and the dark walnut transitional archways helps the merchandise stand out.

Client
  The Limited, Columbus, Ohio

Design Team
  The Limited, Columbus, Ohio – Kathleen Baldwin, director, prototype design; Donna Reilly, director, store design; Bruce Fithian, manager, design standards; Ricky Ney, director, visual merchandising

Outside Lighting Consultant
  Grenald Waldron Associates, Narberth, Pa.

Suppliers
  AEI, Seattle (audio/video); Kravet, New York (fabrics); Retail Fixtures, Racine, Wis. (fixturing); Innovative Marble and Tile, Hauppauge, N.Y., Nemo Tile Co., New York (flooring); Dune, New York (furniture); Carol Barnhart Inc., New York (mannequins); Artglo Sign Co. Inc., Columbus, Ohio (signage); Coszolino, New York (panels); Marlite, Dover, Ohio (puck wall system); Apropos, Minneapolis (plaster finishes)

Photography
  Fred Marsh, Columbus, Ohio

Richards of Greenwich

NEW YORK

Designed to be modern but fit the upscale architecture of Manhattan, the two-story, 27,000-square-foot specialty store features hanging wall panels that serve as flexible space dividers, setting off merchandise lines like jewelry. Men's shoes are merchandised on a cherrywood display wall, characteristic of the masculine, 15,000-square-foot menswear section. The 12,000-square-foot womenswear area is arranged within a creamy off-white color palette around the central atrium upstairs, which provides sightlines to both levels.

Client Team
Mitchells of Westport, Westport, Conn. – Jack Mitchell, ceo; Linda Mitchell, women's buyer and merchandise manager; Russ Mitchell, cfo; Bob Mitchell, vp of men's merchandising

Design Team
Fitzpatrick Design Group Inc., New York – Jay Fitzpatrick, president, creative director; Errol Spence, vp, projects/production; James Robertson, vp, design/decor; Frank Sluzas, project planner; Enrique Montalvo, senior designer; Oscar Adams, project coordinator; Toni Oddo, project decorator

Architects
Herbert S. Newman & Partners, New Haven, Conn. (building architect); Steve A. Lamb Architect, New York (architect of record)

Outside Consultants
Merchandise Lighting Inc., Port Jervis, N.Y. (lighting design); Lewis Baldinger & Son, Astoria, N.Y. (decorative lighting); Old World Iron Inc., Dallas (decorative balustrades); Norris Metal, Brooklyn, N.Y. (perimeter metal work); Crafted Cabinets Inc., Bronx, N.Y. (perimeter/loose fixtures); Altieri, Sebor Wieber, Norwalk, Conn. (mechanical engineering); Tor Smolen Galini & Anastos, New Haven, Conn. (structural engineering); Tritec Building Co., Westport, Conn. (general contractor)

Suppliers
Benjamin Moore Paint Co., Montvale, N.J., Blumenthal, New York, Bendheim Co., New York, Decor Moulding & Supply, Hauppauge, N.Y., Flourishes, New York, Formglas Inc., New York, Jack Lenox Larsen, c/o Cowtan & Tout, New York, J. Robert Scott, New York, Majilite Corp., Dracut, Mass., Maya Romanoff, c/o of Righter Group Inc., Wilmington, Mass., Nevamar, Odenton, Md., Roger Arlington, New York; Tandem Contract, Dayton, N.J., Whittelsey Architectural Wood Sales, Cincinnati (surfaces); Artistic Frame, New York (furniture); Armstrong World Industries, Lancaster, Pa., PermaGrain Products, Newtown Square, Pa., Clodagh Carpets Inc., New York, Innovative Marble & Tile, Hauppauge, N.Y., Masland, New York; Monterey Carpets, New York, Patterson, Flynn & Martin, New York, Roppe, c/o Sales Master, Deer Park, N.Y., Stone Source, New York (flooring)

Photography
Whitney Cox, New York

Guess

CHICAGO

Behind a clean, modern Michigan Ave. storefront, Guess fills its 12,600-square-foot space with men's and women's accessories and clothing. Inside, existing columns are dressed with glossy red jackets to reinforce the brand, adding jaunts of color to the neutral palette. Stone, steel and wood adorns the space, along with stainless-steel framed images and freestanding graphics. Flexible fixturing allows hanging, folded and table presentations.

Client Team
Guess, Los Angeles – Dave Corbin, creative director; Brad Schaefer, retail design manager; Fred Castillo and Matt Morgan, store planning managers; Harry Apter, art director; Robert Higgins, vp of retail development; Brent Saul, director of construction; Michael Kelch, project manager, construction team

Design Firm and Architect
Gensler, Santa Monica, Calif. - Jacek Estoya, John Weidner, Anna Cerlad, Rick McBride, Jeff Henry, Luigi Franceschina, Andy Cohen and Carolina Tombolesi, design team

Outside Consultants
Fisher Development Inc., Des Plaines, Ill. (general contractor); McGuire Engineers and Thornton/Tomasetti Engineers, Chicago (engineering consultants)

Suppliers
AEI, Seattle (audio/visual); Knoll Textiles, Greenville, Pa. (fabrics); Sajo, Montreal (fixturing); John Caretti & Co. Inc., Chicago (poured terrazzo flooring); Andre's Imaging & Graphics, Chicago, Production Photographic, Los Angeles (graphics); Midwest Wholesale Lighting, Los Angeles (lighting); Lifestyle Form & Display Co. Inc., New York (mannequins and forms); Superior Electric Advertising, Long Beach, Calif. (signage); Angela Adams, Portland, Maine (area rugs)

Photography
Micah Smith, Lucky g Photography, Los Angeles

Marshall Field's

CHICAGO

Marshall Field's nearly doubled the original size of its shoe department to almost 34,700 square feet, accommodating 50,000 pairs of shoes. To create a modern, residential feel, the shoes are mostly merchandised on the floor, with several walls reserved for art and furnishings. Stylized light fixtures are arranged throughout the space, and lifestyle merchandising occurs on several full-bodied mannequins dressed head-to-toe – a rarity in shoe departments, noted one of the designers.

Initial Design Conception
Pucci Intl., New York – Phillip Cozzi, design director

Design Team
Houston Wein Associates Inc., Chicago – Jack Houston and Nancy Wein, principals; Jeffrey Stompor, senior designer; Robert Soderholm, project manager

Client Design
The Department Store Div. of Target Corp., Minneapolis – Paul Calderon, design director; Brian Dowd, project coordinator; Jamie Becker, visual coordinator; Len Larson, project manager with Marshall Field's, Chicago

Outside Consultants
Pepper Construction, Chicago (general contractor); Craftsmen United, Milwaukee (perimeter fixture contractor)

Suppliers
Armstrong, Lancaster, Pa. (ceilings); Glant Textiles, Seattle, Donghia Textiles, New York, HBF Textiles, Hickory, N.C. (fabrics); Lees Carpets, Glascow, Va., Emser Tile, Los Angeles (flooring); HBF, Hickory, N.C., and Baker Furniture, Minneapolis (furniture); Maharam, Hauppauge, N.Y. (wallcoverings); Renato Bisazza, Miami (wall tile); Rudy Art Glass, York, Pa. (specialty glass); VenTec Ltd., Chicago (veneers); Wilsonart Intl., Temple, Texas (laminate)

Photography
Susan Kezon, Chicago

Brooks Brothers

SAN FRANCISCO

The Brooks Brothers 16,000-square-foot, two-level San Francisco flagship features off-white limestone flooring and a light, boxy look. The flexible perimeter wall system allows a variety of display possibilities; the workhorse fixture can handle glass shelving or hang-rods. For the first time, women's merchandise has been put at the entrance. Above women's is a floating lightbox in the ceiling, while on the back wall hangs a graphic panel of the retailer's founder.

Client Team
Brooks Brothers, New York – Tom Dougherty, director of design and construction; Lisa Gold, store planning; Paul Sadowski, director of visual merchandising

Design Team
Gensler, San Francisco – Ray Shick, design director; Roy Militar, project manager; Christina Sum, project manager; Jason Jones, Vicky Mitrou, Daniel Scovill, Elinor Tuerk and Rikki Dy-Liacco, design team

Outside Consultants
Revolver Design, San Francisco (lighting); KPFF, San Francisco (structural engineer); Encon, Los Altos, Calif. (MEP engineer); Fisher Development Inc., San Francisco (general contractor)

Suppliers
USG Interiors, Chicago (ceiling); Proco Wood Products, Ossed, Minn. (perimeter fixtures); Hoboken Floors, Wayne, N.J. (wood flooring); St. Marc Claire, distributed by Stone Source, New York (limestone flooring); Harbinger, Atlanta (carpet); Daltile, Dallas (ceramic tile); Armstrong World Industries, Lancaster, Pa. (resilient flooring); La Bruna Industries, Ontario, Calif., and Alpha Display Inc., New York (fixturing); The Retouchables Group Inc., New York (graphics); Indy Lighting, Fishers, Ind., Creative Systems Lighting, Valencia, Calif., Lab Lite, Buffalo, N.Y., Juno Lighting, Des Plaines, Ill. (lighting); Goldsmith, New York (mannequins/forms); Benjamin Moore Paint Co., Montvale, N.J. (paint); Midtown Neon Sign Corp., New York (exterior signage); Zebra Awning, San Francisco (banner)

Photography
Elliott Kaufman, New York

Holt Renfrew

TORONTO

The Holt Renfrew Bloor Street flagship store was designed to re-create the personal-service atmosphere of the 1930s. The women's area is plush and residential, with a kitchen, pantry and marble bathroom, in addition to six private suites for buying clothes with the help of sales associates. The cream and ivory color palette is trimmed with dark wenge wood, as well as feminine aquamarine and rose upholstery. The men's area features a khaki color scheme, mirrored wall and stereo system.

Client Team
Holt Renfrew, Toronto – Anne Walker, vp, construction and design; Tim Wilkinson, store designer; Peter Moore, construction manager

Design Team
Hambrecht Oleson Design Associates, New York – Karen Oleson, creative principal; Argelio Diaz, project manager; Jenna Piccirillo, creative assistant; Debra Robusto, designer

Suppliers
Lee Jofa, New York, C. Duross Ltd., New York (fabrics); Universal Showcase, Clayton, Mo. (fixturing); Sullivan Source Carpet, Toronto (flooring); Louis Interiors, Toronto, Artistic Frame, New York (furniture); Boyd Lighting, New York, Hinson Lighting, New York (lighting); Ebony, Oakville, Ont. (drapery)

Photography
Dub Rogers, New York

Seibu Department Store

TOKYO

The "Summer 2000" displays at the Seibu Department Store in Tokyo breathed life into seasonal fashions by matching stylishly dressed mannequins with colorful, exuberant backdrops. Wild, larger-than-life swirls and feminine shapes suggested movement and rhythm. Some window displays achieved depth with transparent colored film overlaid on the glass.

Client Team
Seibu Department Stores Ltd., Tokyo – Takashi Morita, director; Toshiaki Matuhashi, manager

Design
Hideyuki Taguchi, Tokyo

Suppliers
Takara Shokai Co. Ltd., Tokyo, Kyoei Silk Screen Co. Ltd., Tokyo (props); Patina-V, City of Industry, Calif., Adel Rootstein, London (mannequins); Syunichi Iwaskaki, Tokyo (signage); Tobbie Giddio, New York (illustrations)

Photography
Taku Ohara, Tokyo, and Nobuo Kashi, Tokyo

Seasonal

Although window shopping isn't what it used to be with the rise of suburban shopping malls, holidays provide a great opportunity for downtown retailers to show off their wares. By combining lights, music, graphics, unique materials, props and decoratives, visual merchandisers create their own version of street theater on the retail stage.

And although each year it is hard to believe retailers can outdo themselves, they cull from an endless supply of fairy tales, current events and holiday traditions to create something special. Marshall Field's State Street store breathed life into Alice in Wonderland for one seasonal flower show, while Harry Potter came out to play for Christmas. And perhaps no fictional character captured the joy of changing seasons like Curious George, swinging into the Chicago store for a bit of Spring mischief.

Tiffany & Co.

NEW YORK

For the 2001 holiday season, the historical American jeweler used soft tartan patterns of scarves and bows to represent the "family traditions" theme of its five windows. The first window in the series revealed Mr. and Mrs. Snowman, wrapped in colorful scarves and hats, awaiting their sleigh after a day of shopping for Tiffany jewelry. Stockings filled with Tiffany jewelry and other goodies brightened another scene, and the series was capped with a New Year's celebration in the final window.

Client Design
    Tiffany & Co., New York – Robert Rufino, vp, visual creative
    services and visual merchandising

Photography
    ©Tiffany & Co., Veronica Szarejko, New York

Marshall Field's

CHICAGO

At Marshall Field's, Christmas is all about fulfilling one's wishes. The phrase "Wish Fulfillment," along with a star icon, composed the State Street store's holiday marketing strategy. In the windows, the star appears as ornaments, on hand-sewn pillows, on paintings and in light fixtures.

Client Design Team
    Marshall Field's, Chicago/The Department Store Division of Target Corp., Minneapolis – Donna Milano Johnson, window display specialist; Amy Meadows, visual marketing manager; Jamie Becker, creative director of visual marketing

Photography
    Susan Kezon, Chicago

Myer Melbourne

MELBOURNE, AUSTRALIA

Myer Melbourne, the Australian department store chain, was probably sending a few subliminal messages regarding the virtues of generosity and giving when it presented "A Christmas Carol" in its Bourke Street store. Designed and rendered by Stage One Promotions, a Melbourne production studio, the store presented six animated windows featuring key moments from the Charles Dickens classic. The windows featured architectural models of major buildings that inhabited Melbourne's landscape at the turn of the 20th Century, including a replica of the first Myer store.

Client Design
Myer/Grace Bros., Melbourne, Australia – Mark Reeder, visual merchandising manager

Design Team
Stage One Promotions, Melbourne, Australia – John Kerr, creative and technical director; Andrew Briggs, design and research

Animation
Smart Rigs & Robotics, Melbourne, Australia

Photography
Christopher Howe, Melbourne, Australia

Marshall Field's

CHICAGO

In 11 colorful, animated scenes, Marshall Field's State Street store followed J.K. Rowling's Harry Potter through his life as told in "Harry Potter and the Sorcerer's Stone." The Christmas windows depicted such moments as Harry at the "Mirror of the Erised" ("desire" spelled backwards), where he sees his greatest wish: a family.

Client Design Team
   Marshall Field's State Street, Chicago – Donna Milano Johnson, window display specialist; Amy Meadows, visual marketing manager; The Department Store Division of Target Corp., Minneapolis – Jamie Becker, creative director of visual marketing

Suppliers
   Spaeth Design, New York (window animations); Kinchromize, Chicago, Larson, Tucson, Ariz. (props/decoratives)

Photography
   Susan Kezon, Chicago

The Somerset Collection

TROY, MICH.

The "Once Upon a Time" collection, which is a wily bunch of jesters, made its appearance at the Somerset Collection center in Troy, Mich., as part of a holiday theme. With individually sculpted faces, poseable fingers and an array of energetic postures, the jesters hung from ceilings to catch shoppers' eyes. The figures' clothing was composed of velvets, satins and organza, garnished with beads and silk floral patterns.

Client Team
The Forbes Co., Southfield, Mich. – Nate Forbes, owner; Dave Haysmer, director of operations

Design Team
Panache Designs Ltd., Duluth, Ga. – Pamela Anderson, president; Becky Parker, vp; Ray Dudley, lead designer; Carla Andrews, project coordinator; Jim Robinson, project coordinator

Outside Design Consultants
3-D Creative, Atlanta; Maria Tonelli, Atlanta; Cynthia Wilson, Atlanta; Kevin Nichols, Atlanta; Martha Martin, Norcross, Ga.

Suppliers
Topp Props, Avondale Estates, Ga. (props); Precision Custom Metals, Atlanta (metalwork)

Photography
Mikhail Boutchine, Atlanta

Oscar de la Renta
on 3

Lord & Taylor

NEW YORK

In 2001, Lord & Taylor celebrated its 175th anniversary. The animated windows reflected a rich history of Christmas traditions and how they began. Featured windows included the first White House Christmas tree and the print shop where the first Christmas card was produced. The fashion windows enticed holiday shoppers with a frosty wonderland accented by traditional architectural elements.

Client Design Team
Lord & Taylor, New York – Manoel Renha Rezende, creative director/visual merchandising; Robert Guenste, project manager; Denise Foley, fashion manager; Frank Reilly, senior window decorator; Jessica Grace, Jennifer Johnson, window decorators; Donald Nichols, stock coordinator; George May, painter; Martin Zilari, Kevin McGrath, carpenters

Design
Spaeth Design, New York

Photography
G.M. Pippos, Spotswood, N.J.

Bergdorf Goodman

NEW YORK

A series of white-on-white windows entitled "It's only a dream" delighted the Bergdorf Goodman's shopper for the 2000 holiday season. The store, at the corner of 57th and 58th streets, featured five "Dali-like" dream interpretation windows, packed with all-white merchandise and props, as well as a blizzard of paper sculptures created by the in-house design team.

Client Design Team
Bergdorf Goodman, New York-Linda Fargo, vp of visual merchandising; David Hoey, window director; the Bergdorf Goodman display staff

Photography
Ricky Zehavi, New York

Bloomingdale's

NEW YORK

For the 2000 holiday windows, creative director Michael Fisher and a production team from Swarovski, a European crystal supplier, used crystals and rhinestones to create glittering seasonal sculptures, some of them with animated motion. Sculpted-foam forms, such as a milky white polar bear, cast an opalized shimmer, while Santa and his reindeer gave off a glow.

Client Design Team
    Bloomingdale's, New York — Michael Fisher, creative director; Harry Medina, creative window manager; Adrio Davila, Kevin Burke, Michael Hinojosa, Westwood Papile, design staff

Photography
    Gerald Papillo, New York

Saks Fifth Avenue

NEW YORK

In the six center windows of Saks' store on Fifth Avenue sprouted the story of "Little Tree," inspired by Chris Rahske's book of the same name. The scenes evoked humor and whimsy with a cartoonish Santa, reindeer and conical evergreen trees. Incorporating the triangular shapes present in "Little Tree," the sets were decorated with fabric-filled holiday trees in wood-grain moldings. The other 29 windows balanced the innocence and youth of the primary six, featuring high-end Saks merchandise targeted to specific lifestyles, such as the "ski and spa" customer or the "town and country" customer.

Client Design Team

Saks Fifth Avenue, New York – Sal Lenzo, vp, visual merchandising; Terry Jacobs, New York visual director; James Ranson, lighting designer; Steve Swirczek, fashion manager; Paul Fidler, production manager; Stacey Goldfeder, fashion supervisor; Lars Haga, shop supervisor; Bryan Kollman, production supervisor; Ed Turner, Richard Maynes, Douglas Santos, Koji Yoshioka, Les Hangad, Melodie Provenzano, Sara Schwartz, Kevin Byrnes, Matt Walker, Matt Sullivan, Danny Maloney, Dan Kopp, Robert Nuovo, Joseph Gill, associates

Design Team

Spaeth Design, New York – David Spaeth, Van Craig, Michael Allen, designers

Photography

Gerald Pippos, Spotswood, N.J.

fortunoff

NEW YORK

Fortunoff, the New York jeweler, beckoned spectators to a mechanical "Masked Ball" in its Fifth Avenue windows. Visually choreographed by Ellen Rixford Studios (New York), the windows explored how we reveal ourselves, or use masks. The 35-inch-tall figures were fabricated with mixed media: wood, hard and soft foam, aluminum and wire. Resin was cast very thin for the masks, so they would fit over the faces and not weigh down the heads that rest on the mechanisms.

Client Design
    Fortunoff, New York – Peter Moodie, design director

Design
    Ellen Rixford Studios, New York

Suppliers
    Smooth-On, Gillette, N.J. ("Smooth-Cast" for faces and masks); Chic Fabric, New York, Fabric for Less, New York (costume fabric); Rose Brand, New York (backdrop material)

Photography
    Ellen Rixford Studios, New York

Marshall Field's

CHICAGO

The playful antics of Curious George highlighted one of Marshall Field's festive, seasonal flower displays on State Street. The fictional ape frolicked on his bike, with a kite and with "The Man with the Yellow Hat" in a series of scenes inspired by the children's books. In-store signage also depicted George in trees, swinging above a bright blue "Curious George" carpet that ran through the center of the space.

Client Design Team
Marshall Field's, Chicago/The Department Store Division of Target Corp., Minneapolis – Donna Milano Johnson, window display specialist; Amy Meadows, visual marketing manager; Jamie Becker, creative director of visual marketing

Suppliers
SF Productions, San Francisco (plants, flowers); Larson, Tucson, Ariz. (props, cutouts, animations)

Photography
Susan Kezon, Chicago

"Curious George
Flies a Kite"

"Curious George"

Barneys

NEW YORK

For the 2000 holiday season, Barneys' windows danced to the decades, using live mannequins. Creative director Simon Doonan wanted to acknowledge the popularity of retro fashion and furniture, as well as spoof the rampant voyeurism (e.g., "Survivor") that dominates the airwaves. Ten women from New York's Fashion Institute of Technology were selected to portray hip couples from the 1940s through the 80s, interacting in five window living rooms. The 60s window was filled with references to The Beatles, Twiggy and Bob Dylan, plus Mod and Pop icons were strewn about.

Client Design
    Barneys, New York – Simon Doonan, creative director

Photography
    Ari Mesa, New York

Sony Style

NEW YORK

Christine Belich, executive creative director for Sony Style, took a different approach when deciding upon a holiday theme for 2001. Instead of using elements that would eventually get thrown out, the "Give a Little, Get a Lot" windows used thousands of food, clothing and toy items donated by big companies. These goods, in turn, were donated to charities after New Year's Day. An array of 495 Nike sneakers composed a back wall in one window, as a reindeer made of brown mittens pranced about. A 30-foot tree in the store's atrium was covered in everything from Heinz ketchup to Starbucks coffee packages.

Client Design Team

Sony Style, New York – Christine Belich, executive creative director; Mark Fugarino, graphic designer; LeighAnn Tischler, visual events manager; Ilana Adams, creative coordinator

Suppliers

Rose Brand, New York (fabrics); Sign Solutions, New York, Photobition, New York (graphics); Crosley Customs, San Francisco, Design and Fabrication, New York, Shalem Hughes, New York, McElroy Scenic Services LLC, Millerton, N.Y. (props/decoratives); Eric Brown, New York (illustrations)

Photography

Rick Cadan, New York

David Jones

SYDNEY

Disney heroines lit David Jones' windows on Elizabeth Street for the 2001 holiday season. Snow White, Cinderella, Sleeping Beauty, the Little Mermaid, Belle from "Beauty and the Beast" and Jasmine from "Aladdin" all came to life via sophisticated animatronic systems. Each set represented a storyline from a Disney movie, such as Cinderella at the ball or the kiss from Prince Phillip that awakens Sleeping Beauty.

Client
David Jones Ltd., Australia – Cameron Gordon, visual merchandising manager

Design Team
Stage One Promotions, Port Melbourne, Australia – John Kerr, creative and technical director; Andrew Briggs, design and research

Supplier
Smart Rigs and Robotics, Melbourne, Australia (animation)

Photography
Phoenix Studio, Melbourne, Australia

Henry Birks & Son

MONTREAL

Lucy-Ann Bouwman, visual display consultant from Sightgeist Design (New York), staged an enchanted forest and other assorted fantasies for the Montreal retailer's 2000 holiday windows. Fairy tales were revisited with a modern twist, a la "where are they now?" In an excerpt from a Jack and the Beanstalk vignette, Jack ended up making a fortune in stocks. And Pinocchio's dream of being a TV star (all he needed was a good agent) came true.

Client Design
  Henry Birks & Son, Montreal – Kelly Meadus

Design Team
  Sightgeist Design, New York – Lucy-Ann Bouwman, visual display consultant; Melanie Girdwood, Caroline Thomasset and Patrick Scales, freelance display consultants, Montreal; Multi-Versions Inc., Montreal – Louis LaFontaine

Outside Design Consultant
  Multi-Versions Inc., Montreal – François Trudeau

Suppliers
  Atelier Tweak, Montreal, Sightgeist Design, New York, Multi-Versions Inc., Montreal (props); LSI, Stony Point, N.Y., Dubo Electrics, Montreal, Sightgeist Design, New York (lighting); Sightgeist Design, New York (wallcoverings)

Photography
  Massimo, Montreal

Bergdorf Goodman

NEW YORK

Bergdorf Goodman's serious "Values and Virtues" theme decorated six of its Fifth Avenue holiday windows, each carrying a single title: Hope, Wisdom, Mirth, Friendship, Grace and Beauty. The windows utilized antiques and ornamental fabrics to create an elegant atmosphere. The three 57th Street windows, however, were used to create "A Holiday Card to New York." Wintry, postcard-like scenes, anchored by black-and-white photo collages, depicted familiar New York landmarks and icons.

Client Design Team
   Bergdorf Goodman, New York – Linda Fargo, vp, visual merchandising; David Hoey, window director

Suppliers
   Scalamandre, New York (fabrics/wallcoverings); Newel Art Gallery, New York (furniture); Pucci, New York, Pativa-V, City of Industry, Calif. (mannequins); Duggal, New York (graphics)

Photography
   Ricky Zehavi and John Cordes, New York

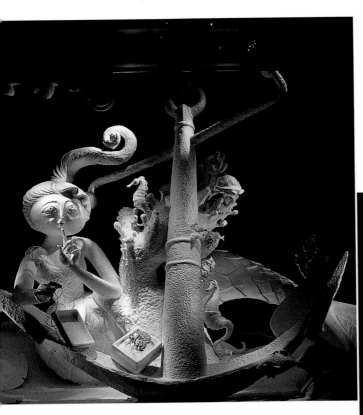

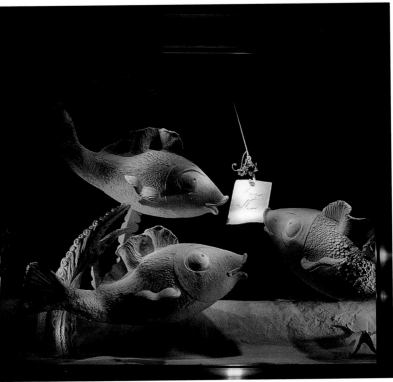

Tiffany & Co.

NEW YORK

For the 2000 holiday season, the legendary New York jewelry house celebrated the season under the sea. Awash in white, dream-like creatures prepared for the holidays. In one window on Fifth Avenue, entitled "Opportunity Presents Itself," a mermaid and fish claimed a piece of a seaweed for their "Christmas tree." They proceeded to decorate it with (you guessed it) jewels. Another window featured a makeshift shell sleigh, adorned with Tiffany's treasures.

Client Design Team
Tiffany & Co., New York – Robert Rufino, vp visual creative services and visual merchandising; John Roccosalva, project manager and artistic direction

Set Construction
Donahue Studios, New York

Supplier
Clint Ross Coller, New York (lighting)

Photography
©Tiffany and Co., Tria Giovan, New York

Lord & Taylor

NEW YORK

Lord & Taylor chose "The Circus is coming to Town" as the theme for the 2000 holiday season, to celebrate the magic and wonder of a child's experience. Clowns, trapeze artists and jugglers danced in the windows, while a neon light sequence heightened the sense of movement. Elsewhere, mechanical performers frolicked beneath a starry fiberoptic sky.

Client Design Team
    Lord & Taylor, New York – Manoel Renha Rezende, creative director/visual merchandising; Robert Guenste, project manager; Denise Foley, fashion manager; Frank Reilly, senior window decorator; Jessica Grace, Jennifer Johnson, window decorators; Donald Nichols, stock coordinator; George May, painter; Martin Zilari, Kevin McGrath, carpenters

Design
    Spaeth Design, New York

Suppliers
    Club 202, New York (music); A. Wimpeheimer & Bros., New York, Circle Fabrics, New York (fabrics); Color Wheel, New York (signage and graphics); Lighting Accessories, New York (lighting); Patina-V, City of Industry, Calif. (mannequins)

Photography
    G.M. Pippos, Spotswood, N.J.

Saks Fifth Avenue

NEW YORK

The New York retailer created a 3-D storyline, starring Little Souls dolls, for the
2000 holiday season. Based on the book,
"One Enchanted Christmas," the six windows presented the story of how Santa
got a new coat in a pinch. The characters
made the garment with the help of
"enchanted" red-velvet drapes. The moving characters were larger than the actu-
al dolls and were given different personalities by sculptor Van Craig of Spaeth
Design (New York).

Client Design Team
    Saks Fifth Avenue, New York – Ken Smart, vp visual mer-
    chandising, Randall Yaw, New York store window director;
    Terry Jacobs, New York store visual and interior director;
    Tim Wisgerhof, New York store production manager;
    Spaeth Design, New York – David Spaeth, principal;
    Michael Allen, designer; Van Craig, sculptor

Photography
    G.M. Pippos, Spotswood, N.J.

"You can't think how glad I am to see you again, you dear old thing!" said the Duchess.

Marshall Field's

CHICAGO

The Marshall Field's State Street team brought Lewis Carroll's "Alice in Wonderland" to life for shoppers during the store's 1999 Flower Show. Thirteen windows featured sets reproduced from the book illustrations, special lighting effects and mechanized characters — including the Caterpillar, complete with a bubbling hookah pipe. In addition to the windows and its traditional storewide bouquets, the store's main aisle was flanked with a procession of trumpet-wielding rabbit guardsmen from the Queen's court.

Client Design Team
Marshall Field's, Chicago/The Department Store Div. of Target Corp., Minneapolis – Jamie Becker, corporate director of visual marketing; Amy Meadows, visual marketing director; Donna Milano Johnson, window display specialist

Suppliers
The Larson Co., Tucson, Ariz. (sets and mechanicals); SF Productions, San Francisco (plants and flowers)

Photography
Susan Kezon, Chicago

holiday hostess gown illuminated by Animotions

DREAM A LITTLE DREAM

Sony Style

NEW YORK

Based on the idea that people love to talk about and dissect the meanings of their dreams, the Madison Avenue retailer staged a "techoliday" display called "Dream a Little Dream." So, the 2000 holiday windows presented a surreal dreamscape inspired by the imaginative REM state. In one window, a "holiday hostess" welcomed everyone to the fantasy. Her gown was created from a fiberoptic material with more than 2.5 miles of animated light. The figure's flashing, beeping head was a sculpture consisting of Sony products.

Client Design Team
Sony Style, New York – Christine Belich, executive creative director; LeighAnn Tischler, visual events manager, New York; Stewart Lucas, visual events manager, San Francisco; Ilana Adams, Shalem Hughes, special consultants; John MacDonald, graphic design

Outside Consultants:
Don Holder Studio, New York (lighting designer); Joseph Domingo, San Francisco (animated dress designer)

Suppliers
Lumin-oZ, Culver City, Calif. (image technology); Malcolm Hill, New York (backdrop illustrations); Eric Brown, New York (painting); Modeworks, New York, TopNotch, New York, Sign Solutions, New York (graphics); Ani-Motion, Bethlehem, Pa. (dress animation); Certerline Studios, Cornwall, N.Y., Brooklyn Design, Brooklyn, N.Y. (props)

Photography
Rick Cadan, New York

Bloomingdale's

NEW YORK

Bloomingdale's 6 windows on Lexington Ave., themed "The Gifts of Christmas," were designed to capitalize on the festivities — such as music, food, gifts and family time — that distinguish the holidays from the rest of the year. Window director Harry Medina wrote the story of three children, lost in the woods after a sled ride, who come across presents in the snow. Using electronic sculptures, the windows depicted the children discovering each gift in a colorful, fantasy-like backdrop.

Client Design Team
Bloomingdale's, New York – Jack Hruska, senior vp, visual merchandising and store design; Joe Cotugno, vp, visual merchandising; Harry Medina, window director, drawings and storyline director

Suppliers
Cooper/Halo Lighting, Peachtree, Ga., Lighting Services Inc., Stoney Point, N.Y. (lighting); Suprina Kenney Studio, Brooklyn, N.Y. (sculptures); Dimensional Lettering, Long Island City, N.Y. (signage); John Langran Studio, Brooklyn, N.Y. (paint finishes); Ginny Walsh Studio, Bayville, N.Y. (motor animation)

Photography
Gerald Pippos, Spotswood, N.J.

Specialty Retail

While department stores provide the convenience of one-stop shopping for consumers with multiple needs, specialty retailers offer consumers a variety of specific merchandise. And unlike department stores, specialty retail shops have the unique opportunity to create a brand-specific environment that revolves around the premier product.

For instance, Steuben crafted a visual merchandising scheme in Manhattan that adds sparkle to its glassware by using brightly illuminated, blue-lined wall cases. The circular mezzanine is even a visual metaphor for the glass-making process, resembling a gather of molten crystal at the end of blowpipe. The Lego Store in Chicago is appropriately fitted with large, colorful sculptures made of its namesake product.

Bloom

NEW YORK

Owner Lesly Zamor needed a new look for his home accessories and flower shop when he moved locations. Janson Goldstein (New York) responded with a clean, serene, nature-based sanctuary. To draw the eye in from the street, warm red Venetian plaster covers one wall, a lively backdrop for the luscious floral bouquets. The wall opposite is sheathed in brushed stainless-steel. Bloom's version of a restaurant's open kitchen is its counter and workstation where flowers are cut and arranged in full view. Poured concrete flooring frames a rectangular reflecting pool, which holds arrangements of water plants.

Client Team
Bloom, New York – Lesly Zamor, owner; Debbie Notis

Design Team
Janson Goldstein LLP, New York – Hal Goldstein, Mark Janson, principals; Peter Weed, project manager

Outside Consultants
Bill Jansing, Dallas (lighting designer); Richter + Ratner, Maspeth, N.Y. (general contractor)

Suppliers
Knoll, Kravet, New York (fabrics); Daniel DeMarco & Associates, Amityville, N.Y. (fixturing); Sterling Upholstery, New York (furniture)

Photography
Paul Warchol, New York

Pottery Barn Kids

COSTA MESA, CALIF.

Pottery Barn Kids bears some of the trademarks of its parent company, Williams-Sonoma: pale columns, merchandising platforms and the look of a design studio. But it's a prototype all its own, featuring washable surfaces and painted Siberian hard pine flooring that makes it kid-proof and easy to maintain. Through a series of bedroom vignettes, starting at the entrance with a seasonal display and ending at the back with Pottery Barn Baby, the simple design comes to life.

Client Team
Williams-Sonoma Inc., San Francisco – Bud Cope, vp store development; David Palachek, design manager, Pottery Barn Kids; Patti Kashima, senior design manager; Liz King, senior project manager, Pottery Barn Kids; Gary Friedman, president

General Contractor
Fisher Development Inc., San Francisco

Design Architect
BCV Architects, San Francisco – Hans Baldauf, Ken Catton, Chris von Eckertsberg, principals; Steve Carter, project manager

Architect of Record
MBH Architects, Alameda, Calif. – John McNulty, principal-in-charge; Rick Nelson, project director; Kris Nelson, design director

Suppliers
Flooring Solutions, Livermore, Calif. (tile); Buddy Rhodes Studio, San Francisco (concrete platforms); Environments, Minnetonka, Minn. (furniture/casework); Richyworks, Los Angeles (conceptual design); Thomas Swan Sign Co. Inc., Philadelphia (graphics); O'Connor Associates, Philadelphia (lighting); Stonehenge, San Francisco (wallcoverings); 3-D Studio, Oakland, Calif. (metalwork)

Photography
Erhard Pfeiffer, Los Angeles

Marcus Rodriguez
Architect

The LEGO® Store

CHICAGO

The LEGO brand made its third stand-alone U.S. appearance with a 5000-square-foot store on Michigan Avenue. Elaborate, hand-made LEGO concoctions appear around the space. To segment the store into different product worlds, mobile fixturing was over-scaled, creating dividers where needed. A light-colored wood offsets the merchandise.

Design Team
LEGO Brand Retail Inc., Carlsbad, Calif. – Carol Stemmerman, vp; Christian Korbes, vp, design and branding; Jeffrey Fields, director of creative design; V.J. Rodrigues, show designer; Jeff Fisher, director of visual design, retail

Outside Consultants
The Cuningham Group, Marina del Rey, Calif. (design); Edwards Technologies, El Segundo, Calif. (audio/video)

Suppliers
Quality Cabinet and Fixture Co., San Diego (fixturing); Compass Display Group, Atlanta, Rose Displays, Salem, Mass. (graphics); Silvestri California, Los Angeles (mannequins); Elevations Inc., S. San Francisco, Calif. (props)

Photography
Karen Hoyt, Chicago

Apartment Zero

WASHINGTON, D.C.

Apartment Zero, selling sleek and iconic furniture and furnishings, specializes in "products for office, home and soul," according to designer and co-owner Douglas Burton. The design provides a witty backdrop to the merchandise: Red walls bring vitality to the interior, while the neutral ceiling, natural wood floors and metallic fixturing infuse urban cool. Colorful banners, visible through the store's windows, give its street presence added punch.

Client Design
Apartment Zero, Washington, D.C. – Douglas Burton, visual display

Suppliers
ALU, New York (fixturing); Parallel Lines, Chicago (furniture); Lightolier, Fall River, Mass. (lighting); Nichols Inc., Salt Lake City (signage)

Photography
Timothy Bell Photography, New York

Crate & Barrel

KING OF PRUSSIA, PA.

Designers customized the dramatic three-story Crate & Barrel building, starting with the front of the store. The structure resembles a ship's prow, with numerous curved and tapered walls of various angles and degrees. The store's interior continues the exterior's blend of masonry block, stucco and cedar siding while also incorporating the retailer's signature whitewashed pine. The "seasonal gallery," which shoppers encounter from either of the two entrances, runs as a main artery through the ground floor. The second floor contains the furniture departments, centered by an open floor-to-ceiling atrium, providing customers with a natural path to follow.

Client Team
Crate & Barrel, Northbrook, Ill. – Jacques Verlinden, director of architecture; Doug Boesen, project architect; Anthony Garippo, director of construction; Richard Stange, project manager

Associate Architect
Good Fulton & Farrell Architects, Dallas

Outside Consultants
Engineering Design Consultants, W. Chester, Pa. (civil engineering); DTI Electric, Huntingdon Valley, Pa. (electric); Williard Inc., Jenkintown, Pa. (HVAC); GeoSystems Consultants Inc., Ft. Washington, Pa. (engineer); Tamburri Associates, Cinnaminson, N.J. (structural engineer)

Construction Manager
Jeffrey M. Brown Associates Inc., New York

Suppliers
Muzak, Seattle (audio/video); American Interior Construction Inc., Newtown Square, Pa. (carpentry); Crate & Barrel, Northbrook, Ill. (fixturing, graphics); Allglass Systems Inc., Pendell, Pa., US Aluminum, Waxahachie, Texas (glass); Creative Architectural Metals, Bensalem, Pa. (handrails); Juno Lighting, Elk Grove Village, Ill. (lighting); AB&S Masonry Corp., Rockledge, Pa. (masonry); Goeblewood Industries Inc., Folsom, Pa. (millwork); Buttonwood Painting, Frazer, Pa. (paint); Kunda Sign, King of Prussia, Pa., City Sign Service Inc., Horsham, Pa. (signage); Creative Finishes, Philadelphia (plaster/stucco); Lower State Tile and Marble, Philadelphia (tile); Flynn Floors, King of Prussia, Pa., DuPont Flooring Systems, Lancaster, Pa., Tembec, Huntsville, Ont. (flooring)

Photography
James A. Evangelista Photography, Collingdale, Pa.

Green

GREENWICH, CONN.

Designers insist that green evokes serenity and is one of the most adaptable colors for home decorating. The 3600-square-foot Green home accessories store features a pale stucco façade, natural bamboo-plank flooring and light-filled cutouts in the interior walls that provide special product niches. Wide concrete stairs draw shoppers to an open, skylit second level. Merchandise is displayed on distressed wooden benches, matte-finished, blackened-steel tables and in polished-glass vitrines.

Client Team
Green, Bedford Hills, N.Y. – Michael Freeman Donohue, owner

Design Team
Franke, Gottsegen, Cox Architects, New York – Norman Cox, Suzana Bellettiere, design team

Outside Consultants
Barrie West, Hereford, U.K. (graphic/logo design); Duo Design, New York (visual merchandising)

Suppliers
RSS Construction Management, Darien, Conn. (construction); Essential Communications, New York (audio); Fleetwood Industries, Reading, Pa. (fixtures)

Photography
Simon Cherry, New York

Ripley's Cargo Hold Shop

GATLINBURG, TENN.

Designers of Ripley's Cargo Hold Gift Shop at Ripley's Aquarium wanted to take visitors' aquatic adventure a step deeper. Taking cues from an element in the aquarium's shark exhibit, JGA Inc. (Southfield, Mich.) designed the gift shop as the cargo hold of a sunken ship. A wall of wood crates functions as the slatwall merchandising system, while oil drums with graphic emblems hold plush merchandise. Porthole display windows, visible from the aquarium side, feature pole systems to merchandise crystal and giftware. And "warning lights" in the children's department act as beacons.

Client Team
Ripley's Entertainment, Orlando – Robert Masterson, president; Robert Kirchgessner, senior project manager; Duffy Mellor, project manager; Leo Shen, vp, merchandising

Design Team
JGA Inc., Southfield, Mich. – Mike Crosson, ceo; Skip West, studio director; Mike Benincasa, creative director; Mike McCahill, project manager; Stephanie Bourdon, creative resources manager; Brian Eastman, graphic design director; Jeremy Grech, project services manager

Architect
HHCP, Maitland, Fla.

General Contractor
Suitt Construction, Greenville, S.C.

Lighting Consultant
Illuminart, Ypsilanti, Mich.

Suppliers
Aged Woods, York, Pa., Lonseal, Carson, Calif., Surface Materials, Solon, Ohio, Armstrong World Industries, Lancaster, Pa. (flooring); Benjamin Moore Paint Co., Montvale, N.J., Rust-Oleum, Vernon Hills, Ill. (paint); Formica Corp., Cincinnati, Wilsonart, Temple, Texas (laminates); Aged Woods, York, Pa. (wood); Cozmyk Enterprises, Columbus, Ohio (millwork)

Photography
Laszlo Regos Photography, Berkley, Mich.

Artefact Design & Salvage

SAN JOSE, CALIF.

A 7500-square-foot former ware-house is home to Artefact Design & Salvage, retailer of high-end architectural elements and garden pieces. The store features high ceilings, open rafters, massive skylights, odd angles and old milling equipment. The biggest visual impact is at the entrance, where customers can look down and see three axes converging. In a store where product is also prop, merchandise is arranged in vignettes, with cast-iron columns marking the space. Unusual dividers, such as shuttered windows and theatrical lighting, highlight other sections and create dramatic, distinct pools of light.

Client Design
Artefact Design & Salvage, San Jose, Calif. – David Allen, owner

General Contractor
Placemakers Inc., Redwood City, Calif.

Outside Consultant
Chris Varrin Lighting Design, Montara, Calif. (lighting)

Suppliers
Dazian Fabrics, Secaucus, N.J. (fabrics); Artefact Design & Salvage, San Jose, Calif. (furniture, props/decoratives, wallcoverings, fixturing)

Photography
John Brennan, Santa Clara, Calif.

Canyon Ranch Living Essentials

LAS VEGAS

The 1200-square-foot boutique centers on a stylized rendering of an aloe plant, while desert tans and grays predominate the space. Dark woods and titanium glass panels add visual interest. Cabinets appear to float above expanses of sauna-style stones, and a 13-foot waterfall adds a calming touch.

Client Team
Canyon Ranch Living Essentials, Tucson, Ariz. – Gary Miner, Robert Smith, Doug Wilson, David Rymark

Design Team
MOVK, New York – Victoria Kirk, Mark Oller, principals; Loren Camilleri, graphic design

Architect
The Stubbins Associates, Cambridge, Mass.

Suppliers/Fabricators
Collings Inc., Las Vegas (millwork); Bendheim Architectural Glass, Passaic, N.J. (glass); Harmonic Environments Inc., Ft. Lauderdale, Fla. (waterfall); Lightolier, Fall River, Mass. (lighting); Reggiana Collection, New Windsor, N.Y. (lighting); Architectural Cathode Lighting Inc., Huntington Park, Calif. (cold cathode lighting); Donghia, New York (fabrics); Prince Street Technologies, Cartersville, Ga. (carpeting); Intertile, San Leandro, Calif. (stone flooring); PermaGrain Products Inc., Newtown Square, Pa. (wood wall paneling); Ann Baderian Ltd., New York (upholstery)

Photography
Michael Plyler, Springdale, Utah

San Francisco Florist & Gifts

SAN FRANCISCO

In the flower section of this shop, customers are encouraged to browse the custom-designed, 117-square-foot walk-in cooler, comprised of steel, maple, glass and illuminated plastic panels. Throughout the space, redwood slats, slate pavers, metal poles and ribbed plastic recall classic outdoor/garden images of fences and patios.

Client Team
San Francisco Florist & Gifts, San Francisco – David Davari and Kamran Akhaven, owners

Design Team:
Huntsman Architectural Group, San Francisco – Keith Turner, project architect; Michael Logue, Sylvia Vojtkova, project team

Lighting Consultant
Janet Nolan, San Francisco

Millwork
Custom Woodcraft, Napa, Calif.

Photography
David Wakely, San Francisco

Wind & Water

NEW YORK

Turning a former pharmacy space into a specialty gift shop required a lot of work, but Horst Design Intl. (Cold Spring Harbor, N.Y.) took the challenge. A dramatic ceiling oculus at the store's center is a focal point to draw customers into the store's long, narrow footprint. The harmonious design takes cues from feng shui principles, noticeable through the store's circulation flow. Adjustable cherrywood shelving on the perimeter was developed to meet the needs of a constantly changing product mix. Rich, natural materials and colors provide a neutral, elegant backdrop to the merchandise.

Client Team
 Wind & Water, New York – Frank Ilagan, Theresa Ilagan, owners

Design Team
 Horst Design Intl., Cold Spring Harbor, N.Y. – Douglas Horst, principal-in-charge; Bernhart Rumphorst, principal, project design; Fidel Miro, director of design and planning; Cynthia Davidson, director of colors and materials; Alex Latham, project architect

General Contractor
 Todwell Construction, Northport, N.Y.

Suppliers
 Blumenthal Inc., Canaan, Conn. (fabrics); Architectural Systems, New York (wood flooring); Stone Source, New York (slate flooring); Store Lighting Systems, New York, Indy Lighting, Fishers, Ind., Lightron of Cornwall, New Windsor, N.Y. (lighting); Formica Corp., Cincinnati, Nevamar, Odenton, Md. (laminates); J.M. Lynne Wallcovering, Ronkonkoma, New York, Blumenthal Inc., Canaan, Conn. (wallcoverings); Robert Doescher Associates, Greenlawn, N.Y., Moderncraft, Northport, N.Y. (fixturing)

Photography
 Elliot Fine, New York

Condom Kingdom

PHILADELPHIA

Condom Kingdom transforms condom purchasing into an adventure. When the nine-year-old store moved to a larger space next door, Dynamic Imagineering (Baltimore) was hired to concoct a castle motif that reflected the store's name. The royal treatment begins with a drawbridge, arched windows, a "sperm-spewing" waterfall and worn-looking cobblestone flooring. Overhead, hand-made plaster "sperm" appear to swim toward an "egg" — actually a dome in a corner of the store. The centerpiece "condom tree" holds the premier product on its leaves, and sperm cells can be found painted onto concrete at the entrance and hanging from chandeliers.

Client
  Condom Kingdom, Philadelphia – Stuart Schlaffman, owner

Design
  John Christinzio Jr. Design Services, Philadelphia

Outside Consultants
  Richard Zeper, Yardley, Pa. (lighting); Coyote Construction, Philadelphia (general contractor)

Suppliers
  Dynamic Imagineering, Baltimore (fixturing/flooring); Miller Lighting, Philadelphia (lighting); Pro Sign, Downington, Pa. (signage)

Photography
  Jeff Fadellin, Philadelphia

So much of who you are...
is revealed by how you live.

Live passionately!

service

Eatons

TORONTO

When Sears Canada decided to renovate its Eatons department store, Toronto-based West 49 Parallel Design was enlisted to handle the Home Fashion departments. The most dramatic change happened at the escalator well, where the floor slabs were cut away on each level to create a funneling effect. Checkerboard-patterned floors and mosaic-tiled niches were used to create visual points of interest throughout. Sensory perception was key in areas like Bath, where blue frosted glass evokes a feeling of freshness and cleanness. Another dominant feature is "talk" or "language" – phrases screened onto lighting fixtures and walls, which supply whimsy and humor to the space.

Client Team
Eatons, Toronto – Kathleen Toman, national design manager; Gary Adamkowski, general manager, store planning and visual merchandising; Greg Paliouras, senior designer, merchandising – Eatons; Placido Dias, general manager, visual presentation, in-store marketing; Rick Sorby, executive vp, marketing

Design Team
West 49 Parallel Design Inc., Toronto – Bev Moroz, president, principal-in-charge; Stanley Kedzierski, vp, principal-in-charge

Suppliers
Canadian Gypsum Co., Oakville, Ont., Armstrong World Industries, Lancaster, Pa. (ceilings); Wm. Prager Ltd., Toronto, J.F. Gillanders, Toronto, C. to C. Group, Orangeville, Ont., Custom Metal Ltd., Toronto, Planit, Toronto, G.S. Woodworking, Toronto, Art Magic, Mississauga, Ont. (fixturing); Architectural Systems Inc., New York, Janastone Consulting, Toronto, Olympia Tile, Toronto, Armstrong World Industries, Lancaster, Pa., Custom Metal Ltd., Toronto, Perfection Carpets, Toronto, Kraus-Melmart Carpets, Mississauga, Ont., Daltile, Dallas, Genuwood-Flortech, Markham, Ont. (flooring); Nelson Garrett, Toronto, Eurolite, Asbury Park, N.J., Lightolier, Fall River, Mass., Eurospec, Toronto (lighting); Metro Wallcoverings, Concord, Ont., Ralph Lauren Paints, New York, Para Paints, Toronto (wallcoverings and paint); Hanson House, Sacramento, Calif. (fountains)

Photography
Design Archive, Toronto

Steuben Glass

NEW YORK

When Steuben Glass decided to open a new, modern flagship on Madison Avenue, designers wanted the glass to dominate the minimalist interior. To celebrate the sparkling qualities of the crystal, stock pieces are displayed on bright blue suede in an illuminated case along one wall. The circular mezzanine level is a visual metaphor for the glassmaking process, resembling a gather of molten crystal at the end of a blowpipe. Engraved crystal on stainless-steel, cylindrical pedestals glow with the subtle blue, mauve and beige color palette.

Client Team
Steuben Glass, a subsidiary of Corning Inc., Corning, N.Y. – Marie McKee, president and ceo; John Youngstrom, project director

Design Team
Ralph Applebaum Associates, New York – Ralph Applebaum, design principal; Jack Pascarosa, project director; Rick Sobel, job captain; Jessica Holbrook, content coordinator; Nadia Coen, graphic designer

Architect
Lockwood Greene, New York

Construction Management
F.J. Sciame Construction Co., New York

Lighting Design
Johnson Schwinghammer, New York

Outside Design Consultants
Scharf Weisberg, New York (audio/visual systems); Showtime Exhibit Builders, Bellmawr, N.J. (fabrication of display units and fixtures)

Suppliers
S&G Woodworking, Brooklyn, N.Y. (millwork); Corcoran Marble, Huntington Station, N.Y. (stone flooring); ASF Glass Inc., W. Babylon, N.Y. (stainless-steel railings, floor lightbox); Wall Track Inc., N. Bergen, N.J. (fabric wall panels); Consolidated Carpeting, New York (carpet installation, entry mat); Blumcraft, Pittsburgh (iron glass, stainless-steel casework and doors); Piik Diemont & Ohl Inc., Bronx, N.Y. (curtain tracks, tracks, drapes)

Photography
Peter Mauss, Esto Photographics Inc., Mamaroneck, N.Y.

SLAPIUS MAGAZEENIUS ANGELUS

Deluxe San Mateo

SAN MATEO, CALIF.

Visual merchandiser Jason Crouch created a promotion for *Slap Magazine*, a
teen-targeted skateboarding publica-
tion, in the window of the Deluxe San
Mateo skateboard shop. The display,
"Angel of Audobon," contained a collage
of the angel decals, as well as a giant
3-D version of the magazine's angel logo.
Pictures of winged creatures from an
Audubon Society desk calendar cover
the wings of the animated-looking
angel. Green alfalfa pellets composed
the flooring, while valve-handles made
sprouting flowers.

Client Design
    Deluxe San Mateo, San Mateo, Calif. – Jason Crouch

Suppliers
    Custom Metals, Belmont, Calif. (metalwork)

Photography
    Jason Crouch, San Mateo, Calif.

Accessories

Accessory retailers often have the most fun with their visual merchandising schemes because of the nature of the product. Accessories complete a look, add a bit of fun and funk, a splash of color or just the right touch to turn an ordinary look into something extraordinary. Likewise, accessory retailers use displays, fixtures, light and color to create dynamic environments out of what are often small spaces.

Take Sonoma Eyeworks, for instance. To showcase its line of eyewear in a 1900-square-foot space, it used custom wall-mounted display cases that optimize storage with mirrored doors to hide additional inventory. Louis Martin Jewelers utilized a round island of showcases to enhance the flow of its square space, as well as a 4-foot-high, 45-foot-long mural that stretches along a curving back wall.

Hard Rock Hotel Retail Store

ORLANDO

References to the glory days of hard rock, like Kiss, loom larger than life in framed supergraphics at the Hard Rock Hotel, Orlando, retail store. The 2670-square-foot space features a circular chandelier crafted of guitars with fiberoptic strings that change color constantly. Behind the proscenium-like cashwrap, velvet "stage curtains" frame a wall of video monitors programmed with concerts from the Orlando concert hall, Hard Rock Live. The cherrywood fixtures, with ebonized wood and wrought-iron detailing, recall the traditional look of Hard Rock Cafés worldwide.

Client Team
Hard Rock Intl. (USA) Inc., Orlando – Craig McIntyre, senior director of design and development; Rick Sconyers, director of design; Craig Scott, project manager; Dianne Hamilton, project coordinator·

Design Team
Retail Planning Associates, Columbus, Ohio - Diane Perduck Rambo, partner; Eric Neiman, strategist; David Denniston, senior art director; Paul Hamilton, senior environmental designer; Dana Fleming, planner/merchandiser

General Contractor
Shawmut Design and Construction, Boston

Soundelux/Showorks, Orlando (audio/video); Rose Brand, New York, Anzea Fabric, Ft. Worth, Texas, Christine Taylor Collection, Doylestown, Pa. (fabrics); Allegheny Millwork, Lawrence, Pa. (fixturing); Verona Marble Co., Dallas, Emser Tile, Los Angeles (flooring); Martin Brattrud, Gardena, Calif. (furniture); Capital Mfg., Lansdale, Pa. (signage, graphics); Sesco Inc., Winter Park, Fla. (guitar chandelier); VenTec Ltd., Chicago (wallcoverings); Sherwin-Williams, Cleveland (paint); Armstrong World Industries, Lancaster, Pa. (vinyl tile); Sherwin-Williams, Cleveland, Phenix Biocomposites, Mankato, Minn., Prismatic Powders, White City, Ore. (special finishes)

Photography
Michael Houghton, STUDIOHIO, Columbus, Ohio

Sonoma Eyeworks

SANTA ROSA, CALIF.

For a distinctively urban look, the 1900-square-foot Sonoma Eyeworks features a dramatic back feature wall composed of wood paneling stained in muted red, yellow and blue. Custom wall-mounted display cases optimize storage and merchandise presentation, with recessed lighting and mirrored doors to hide additional inventory. For drama, the ceiling in the center of the store has been lowered and painted black, and is dotted with MR-16 track lighting.

Client Team
Sonoma Eyeworks, Santa Rosa, Calif. – Jean Fruth, owner; John O'Connell, owner/manager; Linda Guzetti, manager

Design Team
Disrud & Associates, Healdsburg, Calif. – Carol Disrud, president/project director; Robert Meyhaus, project designer; Maritza Almanza, design assistant

General Contractor
Jim Murphy & Associates, Santa Rosa, Calif.

Outside Design Consultant
Nine Design, Healdsburg, Calif. (signage design)

Suppliers
Armstrong Ceilings, Lancaster, Pa. (ceilings); Architex Intl., Northbrook, Ill. (fabrics); Eye Designs, W. Los Angeles, Calif. (fixturing); Hartco, Addison, Texas (hardwood flooring); Patcraft Commercial, Dalton, Ga. (carpet); Nienkamper, Scarborough, Ont. (furniture); Abolite, Cincinnati, Prescolite, San Leandro, Calif., Lithonia Lighting, Conyers, Ga., Columbia Lighting, San Francisco (lighting); Laminart, Pleasant Hill, Calif., Pionite, Auburn, Maine (laminates); Econoline Signs, Santa Rosa, Calif. (signage); VenTec Wood Surfaces, Chicago (wood paneling)

Photography
Lenny Siegel, Healdsburg, Calif.

Louis Martin Jewelers

NEW YORK

Because Louis Martin Jeweler's space is square, with its entrance in one corner, designers outfitted it with a large, round island of showcases bisected by a walkway down the middle. Mahogany and cherry cases are trimmed in stainless steel, while brown and other neutral colors fill out the palette. The focal point of the space is a 4-foot-high, 45-foot-long mural that stretches across a curving back wall. In a style reminiscent of the 1930s, it depicts the diamond's journey from mining to processing, cutting and sorting.

Client Team
Louis Martin Jewelers, New York – Louis Shamie and Martin Mizrahi, owners

Design Team
GRID/3 International, New York – Keith Kovar, principal; Mike Schneider, designer

Suppliers
Foremost Contracting, Brooklyn, N.Y. (general contractor); NJS Carpentry Inc., Union, N.J. (fixturing); Monterey, Santa Ana, Calif. (carpeting); Halo Lighting, Elk Grove Village, Ill., Winona Lighting, Winona, Minn. (lighting); Blumenthal, New York (wallcoverings); Sherwin-Williams, Cleveland (paint); Modeworks, New York (mural)

Photography
Amanda Yates-Hagan, Virden, Man.

Coach

NEW YORK

Modern, geometric wall fixtures at Coach's 6500-square-foot flagship are made using milk-painted pine and mahogany, while freestanding fixtures use ribbed glass and nickel. The luminescent display box, made of opal-white acrylic with a mahogany base, can be adorned with sheets of colored acrylic. A white steel staircase connects the three levels, backed by a white brick wall. Douglas fir end-block flooring keeps the light look grounded, while concealed lighting in every fixture keeps the focus on the product.

Client Team
Coach (a division of Sara Lee Corp.), New York – Coach design team

Design Team
S. Russell Groves, New York – S. Russell Groves, principal; Dan Wismer, project designer; Stephanie Kim, designer; Sun Lee, materials/finishes

Outside Design Consultants
Kugler Tillotson Associates, New York (lighting); Murray Consulting Engineers, Rye, N.Y. (structural engineer); Gabor M. Szakal & Associates Consulting Engineers, New York (MEP)

Suppliers
Rambush Lighting, New York (recessed lighting); Louis Poulsen, Ft. Lauderdale, Fla. (custom pendants); Endicott Brick, New York (glazed brick); Columbia Showcase & Cabinet, Sun Valley, Calif. (fixtures); Haywood-Berk Floor Co., New York (wood flooring); Konstantin Bojanov Projects, Brooklyn, N.Y. (cast-resin build-ups); Bedlam Brass, Garfield, N.J. (custom handrail fabricator)

Photography
Sharon Risedorph, San Francisco

20/20 Optical Store

LONDON

The 15,000-square-foot 20/20 Optical Store flagship offers an extensive product range with an individually tailored customer-service experience. The store is intended to appeal to the customers, but at the same time show its awareness of face-fashion. In the first 15 feet, referred to as the customer "hot zone," designers incorporated a custom-merchandising system that features translucent acrylics. Since the product is small and repetitive, a sophisticated display system and halo lighting in the recessed wall bays puts the focus on the merchandise. Large-scale graphics convey the mission statement message: "Seeing things differently."

Client Design Team
20/20 Optical Store, London – Stephen Isaacs, managing director; Jin Georgiou, operations director

Design Team
20/20 Ltd., London – Vicky Stafford, architect; Justin Starck, graphic designer

Outside Consultants
Into Lighting, London; Abacus, London

Suppliers
Kuadrat Ltd., London (fabrics); Hadleys Shopfitters, Portsmouth, U.K., 20/20, London (fixturing); Floorcraft, London (flooring); HB Contracts, London, Astro Designs, London (furniture); Superchrome, London (graphics/signage); Into Lighting, London (lighting)

Photography
David Barbour, London

Torneau Watch Gear

SHORT HILLS, N.J.

This retail concept for moderately priced watches was designed with young adults in mind. On the perimeter of the glowing 1000-square-foot space are products and graphics displayed on pivoting, two-sided panels attached to the floor and ceiling. Customers can move the panel up to 45 degrees; floor fixtures, fabricated of the same powder-coated aluminum and mint-green frosted acrylic as the panels, can also be reconfigured.

Client Team
Torneau, New York – Bob Wexler, president; Anthony D'Ambrosio, executive vp; Dave Edwards, director of construction and facilities

Design Team
Haines Design Studio, New York – Tobias Haines, Martin Jerry, principals in charge; Sakura Moriya, Stephanie Beeguer, design team

Suppliers
Muzak, New York (audio/video); Gordon Ceilings, Shreveport, La. (ceiling); Triangle Systems, New York (fixturing); Amtico Intl., Atlanta (flooring); RSA Lighting, Chatsworth, Calif. (lighting); Electric Time, Medfield, Mass. (props and decoratives); Alto Signage, Philadelphia (signage); Rise Graphics, New York (scrims)

Photography
Tobias Haines, New York

Lancome Color Studio

SAN FRANCISCO

Because cosmetics retail is moving away from the "traditional glass counter" toward more self-service, Lancome used an illuminated serpentine wall to divide the store into three service zones: a café-style area to target quick-purchase customers and samplers, a more intimate area for full makeovers and an open-sell area. The wall is composed of white plastic laminate with sandblasted-acrylic doors.

Design Team:
Kenne Shepherd, New York – Kenne Shepherd, principal; Patri Merker, New York (associate architect)

Outside Design Consultants
Richter+Ratner Contracting Corp., Maspeth, N.Y. – Lars Nilsen, project manager (contractor); Renee Cooley Lighting Design, New York (lighting); Flack & Kurtz, San Francisco (engineers); Sound & Sight, New York (audio/visual)

Suppliers
Richter+Ratner Contracting Corp., Maspeth, N.Y. (millwork); Cupertino Electric Co., San Francisco (electrical); Metropolitan Glass Corp., San Francisco (glass and mirrors); Tilewest, Berkeley, Calif. (ceramic tile)

Photography
Peter Paige Photography, Upper Saddle River, N.J.

H₂0 Plus

VANCOUVER

The cosmetics company H₂0 Plus decided to revamp its image using a clean, minimalist aesthetic that integrates the blue color of its product range. A feature wall uses frosted and custom cast glass with twin waterfalls, while LED lighting technology creates a vascillating watery backdrop for the store. Gloss-white lacquered finishes complement the custom-colored concrete on counters and floors. Blue gels on the fluorescent tubes and cove lighting provide blue accents matching major product lines.

Client Team
H₂0 Plus, Chicago – Cindy Melk, president; Brad Lenhart, director, communications

Design Team
Architectura Planning Architecture Interiors Inc., Vancouver – Susan Smallenberg, director and principal; D. Brent North, principal; Alan Endall, Philip Gowland, design team

General Contractor
Heron Construction & Millwork Ltd., Richmond, B.C.

Suppliers
Heron Construction & Millwork, Richmond, B.C. (fixturing); AKA Beton, Vancouver (flooring); Architectura, Vancouver (graphics); Color Kinetics Inc., Boston (lighting); Joel Berman Glass Studios, Vancouver, Accuglass, Vancouver (props and decoratives)

Photography
Roger Brooks, Vancouver

Service/Restaurants

Intangible services make up a large part of today's business, from financial services to package shipping. These retail environments must be as attractive and inviting as those designed for tangible products. One company that is doing it right is UPS, with its UPS World Services store in New York. Service representatives don't wait behind counters to accept packages, but walk the floor offering guidance. UPS brown dominates the color palette, while sky-blue wallpaper with clouds add adventurous accent.

From fast food to fine dining, the restaurant business continues to expand. But with a growing industry comes an increasingly fickle and demanding market. Savvy restaurateurs know the recipe for success is an eatery that is appetizing to the eye as well as the stomach.

But theming for theming's sake is, well, so 20th Century. Now, designers take cues from a restaurant's premier product, using color and design schemes that enhance – rather than overwhelm (or worse, disguise) – the quality of the food.

For example, the Il Fornaio Caffe Del Mondo in San Francisco's International Airport features cherrywood and carrara marble to provide a subtly Italian-marketplace feel, reflecting the specialty coffees and baked goods. Chicago's Mod, however, used a near-psychedelic interior and Jetson-like molded plastic chairs to complement the hip American fare.

UPS World Services

NEW YORK

Service representatives roam the floor in this service-oriented venue, helping customers through the shipping process. The familiar UPS brown is featured around the space, such as in the brown MDF counters and earth-colored flooring of cork and sisal. The walls feature sky-blue wallpaper with clouds. A globe icon is prominent in the design, including a large rotating steel-and-copper one found behind a service counter.

Client
United Parcel Service, Atlanta

Design Team
Pentagram, New York – James Biber, Michael Gericke, partners; Michael Zweck-Bronner, associate; James Cleary, Tonya VanCott, architects; Su Mathews, Maggie West, graphic designers

General Contractor
Ambassador, New York

Suppliers
Paul Herbert Woodworking, Torrington, Conn. (cabinetry and fixturing); Pentagram, New York (graphics); Lightolier, Fall River, Mass., Edison-Price Lighting, New York (lighting); Abet Laminati, Englewood, N.J., Formica Corp., Cincinnati (laminates); Dale Travis Associates, New York (signage); Vomela, New York (wallcoverings)

Photography
Andrew Bordwin, New York

eBank

COLUMBUS, OHIO

The "Empowered Banking Experience" exhibit was designed to be a scenario-based marketing tool to promote a "relationship management" software package. Upon entering the space, each visitor would be presented with an ATM card to interact with the various electronic services. Yellow and blue tones dominated the exhibit, with bright, lemon-colored pendant lights punctuating the trademark "e" in the ceiling.

Client Team
eBank, Columbus, Ohio – Paul Jameson, president and ceo; Anita Bodell, Michael Schultz, client advocates

Design Team
Design Forum, Dayton, Ohio

Suppliers
DVS Industries, Burlington, N.J., Kramer Graphics, Dayton, Ohio (graphics); Cassady Woodwork Inc., Dayton, Ohio (millwork); Renovators Inc., Columbus, Ohio (general contracting); Dyna Electric, Columbus, Ohio (electrical contracting)

Photography
Brad Feinknopf, Feinknopf Photography, Columbus, Ohio

MOD

CHICAGO

Riding the wave of enthusiasm for retro modern design, MOD is the brainchild of hip restaurateur Terry Alexander and chef/partner Kelly Courtney. The restaurant's saucy, near-psychedelic interior is the work of London-born designer Suhail, who also creates furniture. He designed the Jetson-like molded-plastic chairs to resemble sliced-off egg cups, colored sky blue or guacamole green. The vestibule is sheathed in bright orange acrylic panels. In the main dining area, circles and squares provide the geometric leitmotif for lighting, fixtures and furnishings. The flooring, which mimics tile, is made of recycled tires.

Client Team
MOD, Chicago — Terry Alexander, Steven Ford, Quay Tao, Kristin Skrainy and Kelly Courtney

Design
Suhail, Chicago

Suppliers
Eco Flooring, London (flooring); Jeremy Lord, London, Dan Streng, Chicago (lighting)

Photography
Doug Fogelson, Chicago

The Greenhouse Spa

NEW YORK

The three-story, 6500-square-foot Spa is described by New York-based architect S. Russell Groves as "a retreat from the city that combines a clean, modern aesthetic with sensuous, tactile materials." At the entrance, a 300-square-foot retail area glows via backlit fabric scrims. Product is displayed on white-lacquered etageres set against oak flooring. The Skylight Café at mezzanine level features cushioned rift-cut oak loveseats, while the 4500-square-foot upper floor houses treatment stations. Flat-screen TVs and sliding oak partitions for private manicures line the space.

Client Team
The Greenhouse Group, Dallas – Gerald and Lee Katzoff, owners

Design Team
S. Russell Groves Architect, New York - S. Russell Groves, principal-in-charge; Rachael Grochowski, project architect; Laura Bernstein, senior designer; Sun Lee, junior designer

General Contractor
Bauhaus Construction, New York

Outside Consultants
Kugler and Suzane Tillotson, New York (lighting); Laslo Bodak and David Rosini, New York (MEP); Frank Fortino, New York (code)

Suppliers
DDM Furniture, New York (furniture/millwork); Stone Source, Manhasset, N.Y. (stone); Kravet, New York (scrim fabric); Ann Sacks Tile, New York (tile); Sohil Mosum, New York (metal fixtures)

Photography
Mark Ross, New York

Qiora Store and Spa

NEW YORK

Sensual materials, diffused lighting and curvaceous forms create a calm, glowing landscape at Shiseido Cosmetics' Qiora Store and Spa in New York. The product glows on display fixtures, illuminated with fiberoptic uplights that cycle through shades of white during the day and blue at night. In the retail section, fabric creates soft boundaries for the consultation and reception areas. In the spa, fabric shrouds the more intimate lounge and cabin areas, where opaque walls are lined with ultrasuede. Light modulates between warm and cool shades to create a sense of daylight and a radiant glow on the skin.

Client Design Team
Shiseido Cosmetics, New York – Aoshi Kudo, designer, creative director; Rikya Vekusa, project manager

Architect
Architecture Research Office (ARO), New York – Stephen Cassell, Adam Yarinsky, partners; Scott Abrahams, project architect; Josh Pulver, Eunice Seng, Rosalyne Shieh, Kim Yao, design team

Outside Consultants
Selnick/Harwood Consulting Engineers, New York (structural); Lilker Associates, New York (mechanical engineer); Johnson Schwinghammer, New York (lighting); Mary Bright Inc., New York (curtains); Shen Milsom, New York, Wilke, New York (audio/visual)

Suppliers
Corragio, New York (organza fabric curtains); Rose Brand, New York (poly chintz curtains); General Polymers, Cincinnati (flooring); A+L Lighting, New York, Lutron, Coopersburg, Pa. (lighting); Opra SGF Associates Inc., New York (fixturing)

Photography
David Joseph, New York

Ursa's Café

ST. LOUIS

Designers developed a gaming theme as the basis for the 7500-square-foot student café. Ursa's signature logo at the entrance consists of individual letters set in three-sided cabinets that rotate via a motor on top. Inside, the space is split into lounge and café areas. A backgammon pattern plays prominently on the walls, hearth and tabletops of the lounge, and on the walls of the adjacent cybercafé. But the attic game room is where patterns play out three-dimensionally: perforated moon patterns enliven one wall, while on another, four layers of security mirrors give the effect of chips falling.

Client Design Team
Washington University, St. Louis – Tim Rogan, project manager; Jim Severine, manager, building services, housing and residential life

Environmental Design and Graphics
Ten8 Group Inc., St. Louis – Heather Testa, Dawn Jungermann, Jonathan Bryant, Hector Ciazza, Nancy Compas, Deb Pilutti, Matt McInerney, Grant Gibson, design team

Architect
Mackey Mitchell Associates, St. Louis

Suppliers
Engraphix, St. Louis, Star Signs & Graphics Inc., Lawrence, Kan. (signage/graphics); Midwest Marketing, Peoria, Ill. (installation of window film in Cyber Café); Artfull Tile & Mirror, St. Louis (mirrored wall)

Photography
Barclay Goeppner, St. Louis

Ajune Day Spa

NEW YORK

The Ajune Day Spa features a bold, inspiring design that imparts a sense of peace and equilibrium upon arrival. Polished concrete flooring at the entrance is outlined by mosaic glass tiles, a processional encouraging exploration through the space. The custom-crafted cabinet walls are referred to as the "Informational Forest," displaying products and information throughout. Spa seekers must navigate the "Hall of Whispers" to reach the treatment rooms. This elongated, glowing, etched-glass passageway is marked by the sound of falling water.

Client
Ajune Day Spa, New York – Dr. Mauro Romita, owner

Architect
Robert D. Henry Architects, New York – Robert Henry, principal; Nicole Migeon, project architect; Adam Koffler, Daniela Reboucas, design team

Suppliers
Corragio, New York (curtain fabric); Startup Metals, Pondridge, N.Y. (metalwork); Shaw Commercial, Dalton, Ga. (carpet); GL Lites On, New York (custom lighting); Richmond Ceramic Tile, Staten Island, N.Y. (ceramic tile); Oceanside Glasstile, Staten Island, N.Y. (mosaic tile); The Interiors Group LLC, Lodi, N.J. (millwork)

Photography
Dan Bibb, New York

Hollywood Video

POLAND

A chain of Hollywood Video stores in Poland is intended to bring some Southern California warmth to the Eastern European retail landscape. The prototype store plan is circular, with shelves radiating from a round information desk built around a 3-D version of the palm tree logo – featuring a strip of film for a trunk.

Design Team
    Pentagram, New York – James Biber, partner/architect; Woody Pirtle, partner/graphics; Michael Zweck-Bronner, associate/architect; John Klotnia, associate/graphics; Tanya Van Cott, architectural team; Orville Kaiser and Seung-Il Choi, graphics team; Deborah Short, project coordinator

Photography
    Peter Cook, view pictures ltd., London

| service/restaurants |

Office Pavilion

SAN DIEGO

The 38,000-square-foot office furniture showroom known as Office Pavilion also functions as an education center, furniture gallery and working office space for employees of the Southern California manufacturer's rep sales firm. Conference and office spaces are defined by freestanding "houses." Instead of traditional drywall, clear plastics and PVC piping delineate the interior, based on a color palette of red, black, gray and green. Flooring is striped maple and ash, intersected by striped carpeting.

Client
Office Pavilion, San Diego – Vicky Carlson, president

Design Team
The McCulley Group LLC, Solana Beach, Calif. – Jaime Laurella, Ane Rocha, project managers; John McCulley, principal-in-charge; Julia Spengler, Gretchen Leary, Alan Robles, graphic design team

General Contractor
Johnson & Jennings, San Diego

Suppliers
ATP Graphics, Santee, Calif. (signage); Herman Miller Furniture, Zeeland, Mich., HBF Furniture, Hickory, N.C., Davis Furniture Industries Inc., High Point, N.C. (furniture); Shaw Contract Carpet, Dalton, Ga. (carpet); PermaGrain Products, Newtown Square, Pa. (lobby flooring); Armstrong World Industries, Lancaster, Pa. (resilient flooring); Roppe Corp., Fostoria, Ohio (base); Mechoshade Systems Inc., Long Island City, N.Y., Pollack & Associates, New York, Brentano, Northbrook, Ill. (window coverings); Abet Inc., Englewood, N.J., Formica Corp., Cincinnati, Nevamar, Odenton, Md., Lamin-Art Inc., Elk Grove Village, Ill. (surfaces); Arizona Tile, Tempe, Ariz. (marble transaction counter); Blumenthal Inc., Canaan, Conn., HBF Furniture, Hickory, N.C., Herman Miller, Zeeland, Mich. (fabrics); Elliptipar, W. Haven, Conn., Halo Lighting, Elk Grove Village, Ill., Linear Lighting Corp., Long Island City, N.Y., Lucifer Lighting Co., San Antonio, Texas, Metalux, Elk Grove Village, Ill., Portfolio, Elk Grove Village, Ill. (lighting); Blumenthal Wallcovering, Canaan, Conn., Carnegie Fabrics, Rockville, Centre, N.Y. (wallcoverings)

Photography
Marvin Rand Associates, Venice Beach, Calif.

frisch's

BATAVIA, OHIO

When Frisch's Big Boy decided to revamp its look, it wanted to retain the nostalgia associated with the chain's trademark double-decker sandwich and recognizable statue. The most notice-able design feature is a signature glass-block entry tower that resembles a glowing salt shaker, illuminated with kinetic lighting. Designed to be casual for younger consumers, the café is marked by whimsical materials with a contemporary twist. Confetti tile, metal chairs and an undulating ceiling element mark the open, airy space. In the dining room, dark-wood booths with horizontal porchboard and glass partitions create a more intimate feel, as does the checker-board-patterned carpet.

Client Team
Frisch's Big Boy, Cincinnati – Craig Maier, ceo; John Hunter, vp, property development; Karen Maier, vp, marketing

Design Team
FRCH Design Worldwide, Cincinnati – Thomas Horwitz, principal-in-charge; Steve McGowan, vp/creative leader, senior interior designer; Tessa Westermeyer, vp/communications leader, senior graphic designer; Rebecca Stillpass, brand consulting; Mason Proudfoot, project manager; Bill Bily, graphic designer; Larissa Thayer, visual merchandising

Suppliers
Mannington Commercial, Calhoun, Ga. (carpet); Daltile, Dallas (tile); Smith & Noble, Corona, Calif. (window treatments); Armstrong World Industries, Lancaster, Pa. (ceiling); Maharam, Hauppauge, N.Y. (fabrics); Benjamin Moore Paint Co., Montvale, N.J. (paint); Nevamar, Odenton, Md., Wilsonart, Temple, Texas (plastic laminates); Marlite, Dover, Ohio (wall panels); Stylmark, Minneapolis (architectural trim); Advanced Technology, Greensboro, N.C. (metal laminate)

Photography
Mark Steele Photography, Columbus, Ohio

Shisheido

NEW YORK

The 38,000-square-foot, 2-level "interactive beauty and wellness learning center" communicates luminosity, with white-on-white décor. The space includes a wellness conference center and a pair of private "cabinets" for in-depth beauty therapies. The linear eastern wall has a quartet of semi-private alcoves – defined by demi-walls of frosted water-white glass topped with lintel panes – for skin-care consultations. The back, dedicated to fragrances, features a "pinched" entry and an LED lighting system for color washes.

Design Team
1100 Architect, New York – Juergen Reihm, principal; Antonia Kwong, project captain; Erica Freidland, Yeekai Lim, Selin Maner, Kris Mun, Philip Speranza, design assistants; Julia Bensiek, Dorothy Ollesch, model makers

General Contractor
Taocon Inc., New York

Suppliers
Timeless Plaster, New York (plaster walls); ATTA Inc., New York (resin counters); PPG Starfire, Pittsburgh (specialty glass); Hanover Pavers, Hanover, Pa. (flooring); IDMD Manufacturing, Toronto (display trays)

Photography
Paul Warchol Photography, New York

service/restaurants

Il Fornaio Caffe Del Mondo

SAN FRANCISCO

Il Fornaio America is known for projects that emulate Italian marketplaces. But BCV Architects (San Francisco) also incorporated bold iconic architectural touches and traditionally elegant materials into the Caffe Del Mondo design, such as cherrywood and carrara marble. Two Caffes exist at the San Francisco Intl. Airport: a wine bar with a counter for specialty coffees and baked goods; and a more elaborate facility with tables.

Client Team
D-Lew Enterprises, San Francsco – Darren Lewis, Scott Roderick, Carmen Mayo, Michael Levine

Design Team
Baldauf Catton Von Eckartsberg (BCV Architects), San Francisco – Chris von Eckartsberg, Hans Baldauf and Ken Catton, design principals; Brian Milford, project manager/architect

General Contractor:
Terra Nova Industries, Walnut Creek, Calif.

Suppliers
Architectural Woodwork of Montana, Columbia Falls, Mont. (fixturing); Thonet, Statesville, N.C., EmuAmericas, Bridgeport, Conn., Shelby Williams, San Francisco (furniture); RDG Designs, San Francisco (graphics); Luce Contract/Neidhartdt Lighting, San Francisco, Benya Lighting Design, W. Linn, Ore. (lighting); Bill Moore & Associates, Albany, Calif. (signage); Chalktalk, Long Beach, Calif. (menuboard); Duracite, Benicia, Calif. (stone); Eclipse, Point Richmond, Calif. (metalwork); Harrison Koellner LLC, S. San Francisco, Calif. (food service)

Photography
J.D. Peterson, San Francisco

Branding/Signage/Graphics

Signage, graphics and collateral material are important aspects of great design and visual merchandising. An attractive, clever, clear and concise visual graphics system takes the guesswork out of store navigation, guiding customers toward specific categories and bringing cohesiveness to a brand.

A Fubu shop in Macy's Herald Square took cues from the music industry — an image the company seeks to cultivate — with an exposed sound system protected by a Plexiglass® shield. A prominent tiered table featured two canted Corian ends, suggesting the mark of victory, part of the brand's sporty identity. 3-D displays and vacation-settings vignettes worked best for Samsonite World of Travel in McLean, Va. A Rand McNally map center and sailboat imagery add to the brand's feel of adventure.

XX XY

TORONTO

The 12,000-square-foot jeans and sports-wear store is targeted toward those aged 16 to 29, combining brands such as Fubu, Diesel, DKNY (and of course XX XY) under one roof. Gene imagery reinforces the core brand, while scrims differentiate the retailer from nearby competitors like Urban Outfitters. Stainless steel and wood materials are set against white floors and walls, while large-format graphics identify the target consumer.

Design Team
Yabu Pushelberg, Toronto – George Yabu, creative director; Glenn Pushelberg, managing partner; Andrew Kimber, construction coordinator, designer; Sanjit Manku, designer; Mehari Seare, technical leader; Alex Edward, Shane Park, technical team

General Contractor
Yustin Interiors Ltd., Mississauga, Ont.

Suppliers
Provincial Store Fixtures Ltd., Mississauga, Ont. (millwork); Vogue Display, Toronto (metal); Sunset Neon, Burlington, Ont. (signage); Metromedia Technologies Intl. Inc., Los Angeles (scrim); Stonehard Canada, Whitby, Ont. (flooring); TPL Marketing Inc., Concord, Ont. (lighting); Entertainment Technology, Toronto (entertainment/electric consultant)

Photography
Evan Dion, Toronto

PlayStation 2

LOS ANGELES

This 44,000-square-foot exhibit booth at the Electronic Entertainment Expo featured 3-D computer game characters and props. A large Jumbotron screen split in two to reveal a theater's tunnel entry, while 170 computer kiosks filled the environment. Lit signage illuminated the space.

Client Team
Sony Computer Entertainment America, Park Ridge, N.J. – Marilyn Weyant, vp, loyalty and channel marketing; Ed DeMasi, director, creative services

Design Team
Mauk Design, San Francisco – Mitchell Mauk, principal-in-charge; Adam Brodsley, Laurence Raines, Christiane Forstnig, James Pennington-Kent, design team

Suppliers
Pinnacle Exhibits, Hillsboro, Ore. (signage and principal fabricator); Richanbach & Associates, Millbrae, Calif. (audio/visual); Moss Structures, Portland, Maine (fabrics); Lonseal Inc., Carlson, Calif. (flooring); Chroma Copy, San Francisco, Photobition, San Francisco (graphics); John Osborne, Merced, Calif. (lighting); Dillon Works! Inc., Mukilteo, Wash. (3-D elements); Innovations in Wallcoverings Inc., New York (wallpaper)

Photography
Andy Caulfield, Needham Heights, Mass.

Club Libby Lu

CHICAGO

Club Libby Lu is aptly described by its tagline: "It's a girl thing!" The club, which sells makeup, costumes, jewelry and lotions to pre-teens, achieves glittering success in both its packaging and display concepts. The playful pink and purple logo is a crowned heart with "Club Libby Lu" marching across the front. For small purchases, royal-looking paperboard purses replace shopping bags.

Client Team
Club Libby Lu, Chicago – Mary Drolet, ceo; Erin Killoran, executive vp

Design Team
Chute Gerdeman, Chicago, Columbus, Ohio – Lee Peterson, Jennifer Linn, brand development; Debra Thuma, program manger; Brian Shafley, creative director/AE; Lori Mukoyama, senior designer; Adam Limbach, graphics designer; Tina Burnham, graphic production manager; Susan Siewny, Steve Boreman, graphics production; Glennon Schaffner, design development

Outside Consultants
RAS Builders, Chicago (general contractor); Ridgeland and Associates Architects, Oak Brook, Ill. (architect)

Suppliers
Creative Solutions Intl., Scandia, Minn., EPS Specialties, Cincinnati (fixtures); Amtico Intl., Atlanta, Atlas Carpet Mills, Los Angeles (flooring); Andre's Imaging & Graphics, Chicago, MK Signs, Chicago, Belltown Boxing, Seattle, Howard Packaging, Lincolnwood, Ill. (signage/graphics); Lighting Management, New York (lighting); Ian Crawford Fabrics, Palm Springs, Calif., Knoll Textiles, New York, Naugahyde, Soughton, Wis. (textiles); Anton Kobrinetz Design Inc., Chicago (furniture); Abet Laminati, Englewood, N.J., Pionite, Auburn, Maine, Chemetal, Easthampton, Mass. (laminates); Scuffmaster, Minneapolis, ICI/Dulux, Cleveland, Sherwin-Williams Co., Cleveland, Duron Paints & Wallcoverings, Beltsville, Md. (paint); Server Products, Menomonee Falls, Wis. (pumps); Yankee Containers, New Haven, Conn. (glass containers); Fasteners for Retail, Solon, Ohio (decorative hardware); Ample Plastics Co., Wyoming, Mich. (acrylic frames)

Photography
Mark Steele Photography, Columbus, Ohio (graphics and packaging shots); Michael Roberts, Chicago (store shots)

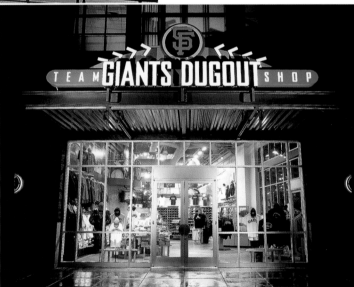

San Francisco Giants Dugout Store

SAN FRANCISCO

The San Francisco Giants wanted a team shop that would entice fans to shop and buy as they passed through to the ballpark. The 5000-square-foot, two-floor Dugout Store features a 6-foot-high band of wallpaper graphics, featuring historical images of Giants teams throughout the years. Repetition of the team logo, graphics and pennants also reinforces the Giants' team brand. Because of the limited floor area, designers took advantage of the high ceilings and tall billboard display walls, and created layers and tiers of both graphics and merchandise to emphasize the product.

Client Team
  San Francisco Giants – Connie Kullberg, general manager, retail and Internet; Derik Landry, director, retail operations

Design Team
  Callison Architecture Inc., Seattle – George Wickwire, principal-in-charge; Martin Anderson, design principal; Stephanie Long, designer; Ron Singler, graphic design; Xiaolei Ouyang, construction administration

Suppliers
  Gerbert Ltd., Lancaster, Pa. (flooring); Comatec, Toronto (store fixtures, cashwraps); Supergraphics, San Francisco, Thomas Swan Co., San Francisco (graphics/signage); Abolite, Cincinnati, Holophane, Richmond Hill, Ont., Juno Lighting, Des Plaines, Ill. (lighting); Kovach, Mesa, Ariz., Benjamin Moore Paint, Los Angeles (wallcoverings)

Photography
  Chris Eden, Seattle

WHSmith books.co

PITTSBURGH

WHSmith books.co in Pittsburgh Intl. Airport's Airmall™ is set up in a 1400-square-foot, post-modern environment, specially tailored for the traveler on the go. Bookmachine.com, a touch-screen book-vending concept, is incorporated into the storefront, allowing customers to purchase a bestseller no matter what the time. Colorful, wayfinding signage makes it easy for shoppers to find the books they seek. Design elements such as the pearlized blue-red storefront finish, ocean-colored tile and hardwood flooring, along with beechwood fixtures trimmed in brushed steel, contribute to the store's upscale, contemporary feel.

Client Team
WHSmith USA Travel Retail (WHSmith international design team), Atlanta – John Cugasi, brand director; Debbie Thompson, construction director, Rebecca Gadbois, interior design manager; Robyn Bilbrey, marketing services manager; William Turner, infrastructure, MS manager

Design Team
FRCH Design Worldwide, Cincinnati – Beth Neroni Harlor, vp, specialty retail; Jeffrey Sackenheim, project manager/architect; Shane Cavanagh, director, architecture; Fitch, London, WHSmith Internal Team, Atlanta (preliminary concept)

Outside Consultants
Lighting Products, Atlanta (lighting); Anderson Art and Design, Waleska, Ga. (graphics); Parkway Imaging, Chicago (interior signage); Shannon Construction, Pittsburgh (construction contractor)

Suppliers
MEI Digital Ltd., London (audio/visual); IBM, Armonk, N.Y. (computer monitors); Fujitsu, Tokyo (plasma screens); Apex Woodworks, Toronto (fixturing); GranitiFiandre, Itasca, Ill. (floor tile); Wilsonart Intl., Temple, Texas (laminate flooring); Parkway Imaging, Chicago (graphics, custom wallcoverings); Alico Industries, Toronto, Juno Lighting, Des Plaines, Ill., Seagull Lighting, Riverside, N.J. (lighting); Precision Plastics, Hiram, Ga. (props/decoratives); Gordon Signs, Denver (exterior signage); Ineos Acrylics, Peachtree City, Ga. (custom lightboxes)

Photography
Kevin Cook, Graule Studios, Pittsburgh

Cherry Creek Shopping Center

DENVER

It's a party! Cherry Creek Shopping Center celebrated its 10th anniversary with plum and pink outdoor banners and corresponding collateral, including stationery and tenant party invitations. Brightly colored images of happy, jumping people appeared on the mall signage, and $10,000 shopping sprees were given away at the end of the promotion.

Client Team
    Lisa Herzlich, marketing director; Liza Prall, project coordinator

Design Team
    Ellen Bruss Design, Denver – Ellen Bruss, owner

Suppliers
    Precision Litho, Salt Lake City, Utah (graphics); Eye Candy Graphics, Denver, Colo. (signage); Nichols, Salt Lake City, Utah (banners)

Photography
    Courtesy of Ellen Bruss Design, Denver

fubu

NEW YORK

Fubu's first retail venture, as a vendor shop in Macy's Herald Square store, was designed to communicate a lifestyle of hip-hop and sports. The shop featured an exposed sound system protected by a Plexiglas® shield, as well as a display wall divided into 30-inch blocks, with wider hangers so oversized apparel could hang freely. The custom fixturing was black, silver and lacquer-red, such as the tiered-table cashwrap with two canted Corian® ends, suggesting the mark of victory.

Client
    Fubu, New York – Daymond John, ceo

Design Team
    Brand Environment (BE) Partners, New York – Debra Post, partner; Paul Bennett, partner; Debbie Sansevero, partner; Kevin Law, Lisa Wright, Allison Turner, design team

Outside Design Consultants
    Johnson Schwinghammer, New York (lighting designer); IBEX Construction, New York (general contractor)

Suppliers
    Dru Whitacre Media Services, New York (audio/video); Encore Retail Systems, Brooklyn, N.Y. (fixturing); Architectural Systems Inc., New York (flooring and Corian supplier); DuPont, Wilmington, Del. (Corian); Buell Wood Flooring, Dallas (flooring manufacturer); Big Apple Sign, New York (signage and graphics); Greneker, Los Angeles (mannequins/forms)

Photography
    David Joseph, New York

Samsonite World of Travel

MCLEAN, VA.

Customers are drawn into the 5200-square-foot space by several vignettes that combine 3-D displays, lights and sound to showcase different vacation settings with luggage displays. One of the many in-store service features is the "Travel Partner," a third-party travel agency. Such stations feature comfortable seating and room for customers to refer to books or maps.

Design Team
Grid 2 Intl., New York – Martin Roberts, president; Akka Ma and Betty Chow, vps; Jeffrey Cook, graphics associate; Steven Derwoed, director of projects; Jennifer Staab, Jayson Chevere, Warren Castellani, designers

Suppliers
Spectrum Displays Inc., Tiverton, R.I. (fixturing); Duggal, New York (graphics); Essential Communications, New York (audio); Shaw Contract Flooring, Weymouth, Mass. (flooring)

Photography
Alan Karchmer, Washington, D.C.

Gerald Stevens

FT. LAUDERDALE, FLA.

Gerald Stevens, a floral retailer based in Ft. Lauderdale, Fla., is modernizing its facilities as a first step toward developing a national brand. Along with the new store, Retail Planning Associates of Columbus, Ohio, created a wide range of collateral materials. The company's new brand mark — a delicate leaf — appears on gift bags, brochures, business cards, stationery and newsletters.

Client Team
Gerald Stevens, Ft. Lauderdale, Fla. — Gerry Geddis, president, ceo; Steve Berrard, chair; Ellie Callison, senior vp, chief marketing officer; Stephanie Carlomagno, vp store planning, visual merchandising

Design Team
Retail Planning Associates (RPA), Columbus, Ohio - Doug Cheesman, ceo; Diane Perduk Rambo, executive senior vp/officer in charge; Jane Thompson, vp; Aaron Spiess, account executive; Nicholas Baughman, senior merchandiser; Kurt Shade, environmental designer; Johnna Castle, materials and finishes; Jennifer Brungart, graphic designer; Mark Holman, lighting designer; Jamie Soteriades, project coordinator; Pat Heinzman, project director; Tonya Passarelli, retail strategist; Dave Spurbeck, documentation specialist; Kathy DiMascio, junior graphic designer; Jim Penn, planner; Dan Poor, director of production management

Photography
Michael Houghton, Studiohio, Columbus, Ohio

H&M

NEW YORK

The Swedish retailer's three-story, 35,000-square-foot American flagship features a light-flooded central atrium linking the three selling levels. An X-shaped escalator carries shoppers from the "trends" department at ground level to the men's department and then ladies' on level three. "Trends" is punctuated by a procession of mannequins positioned on a catwalk-like riser. Brushed stainless steel, white-lacquered MDF and mirrored glass compose the open-sell custom fixturing of the in-house line of cosmetics.

Client Team
H&M, Stockholm, Sweden – Ulrika Sjoberg, project designer; Tommie Stalkula, director of construction; Eivor Haadas, display support specialist

Design Team
The Phillips Group, New York – Michel-Claude Fiechter, principal-in-charge; Steven Segure, project manager; David Fleming, project designer; George Rosa, project architect; Melissa Baker, job captain

Outside Design Consultant
Focus Lighting, New York – Alex Sheshalmi, designer

General Contractor
Barney Skanska Construction Co., New York – Joseph Cicione, Richard Christ

Cleint Representative
Quatararo & Associates, New York – Richard Jantz, Eric Wagner

Suppliers
Thorton-Tomasetti, New York, Ambrosino Depinto Schneider, New York, Milrose Consultants, New York (engineering); Pioneer New Media Technologies, Long Beach, Calif., Sharp Electronics, Mahwah, N.J. (plasma and LCD screens); Bose Corp., Framingham, Mass., ECI Communications, S. Plainfield, N.J. (sound systems); Jasco Industries, Central Islip, N.Y. (display fixtures and millwork); ALU, Milan (cosmetics and toiletries fixturing); Boa-Franc, St. George, Que. (wood flooring); Mats Inc., Stoughton, Mass., Carousel Carpet Mills, Ukiah, Calif. (carpeting); Daltile, Dallas (ceramic tile); Clay-Paky, Lombardy, Italy, Electronic Theatre Controls, Middleton, Wis., Zumtobel Staff Lighting, Highland, N.Y., RSA Lighting, Chatsworth, Calif., Elliptipar, W. Haven, Conn., A&L Lighting, Medford, N.Y. (lighting); Rootstein, New York (mannequins); Certified Graphics, Medford, N.Y. (signage and graphics); Coordinated Metals, Carlstadt, N.J. (stainless steel)

Photography
Peter Mauss, Esto Photographics, Mamaroneck, N.Y.

Great Lakes Crossing

AUBURN HILLS, MICH.

Great Lakes Crossing near Detroit is a 2-million-square-foot retail property with nine separate "districts," each depicting an aspect of Michigan's outdoor lifestyle. Communication Arts developed interior design elements, including signage and graphics, to reflect the outdoor theme. Steel entrance arches with cut-out letters provide distinct graphic identities for each district, and the 1000-seat food court features huge channel-letter identity signs hung from the skylit ceiling.

Client Team
  The Taubman Co., Bloomfield, Mich. – Ron Loch, design development director; Bob Tremonti, vp, planning and design; Jeff Armitage, vp, construction; Scott McArthey, development director; Mike Moukallan, construction director

Design
  Communication Arts Inc., Boulder, Colo.

Photography
  R. Greg Horsley, Austin, Texas

Displays/Fixtures

With an increasing variety of merchandise available in stores, point-of-purchase and informational displays have never been so important. Customers faced with a sea of merchandise will naturally gravitate toward displays that offer guidance on choosing products.

As such, retailers recognize the important roles point-of-purchase displays and fixtures play in a design scheme. While overall design creates a unique and visually interesting backdrop for a retailer's entire product range, displays can be used to highlight a hot product, or draw attention to flagging or discounted merchandise. They are also great tools for educating, entertaining or performing other interactive functions that take the guesswork out of product selection.

At Richards of Greenwich, hanging panel walls serve as flexible space dividers, also setting off jewelry lines like David Yurman in white-lined cases. Pittsburgh's Creative Kidstuff highlighted its colorful gadgets with colorful floor fixtures and nesting tables, some dividing merchandise via built-in plastic bins. The fixtures' whimsical, curvilinear shapes match the toys perfectly.

Nordstrom

BUFORD, GA.

To separate women's apparel areas into two main zones – classic/mainstream and modern/forward – Nordstrom created boutique environments within the zones to emphasize corresponding brands. White sculptural scrim creates a stage that emphasizes mannequins in the modern zone by the escalator, featuring a "Reinvent Yourself" tagline. Theatrical columns and funky furniture abound. In the classics zone, a walnut palette includes armoire-like fixturing for a residential feel.

Client Design Team
Nordstrom Store Planning and Architecture, Seattle – Dave Lindsey, vp; Susan Morton, director of interior design, concepts; Nancy Webber, manager of interior design, concepts; Paige Boggs, Clint Kendall, Tim Rausch, project team

Architect
Callison Architecture, Seattle – M.J. Munsell, principal, design direction; John Bierly, principal; Arthur Teller, architect, project manager; Diane Emick, interiors project manager; Doug Shaw, interior designer; Karen Oshiro, project architect; Dave Brown, Tina Negri, Christian Jochman, Erin Krohn, Barbara Grubb, Curtis Hughes, Ron Singler, Kelly Earls, Barry Shuman, Annette Hillesland, department design

Outside Design Consultant
Juicy Lime Design, Seattle – James Aitken, principal designer (lighting)

Suppliers
Leibold Communications Inc., Seattle (audio); Armstrong World Industries, Lancaster, Pa. (ceiling); Design Tex Fabrics, New York, Donghia Textiles, New York, Pollack & Associates, New York, Giant Textiles, Seattle (fabrics); Ardex Inc., Caraopolis, Pa. (concrete); Pacific Coast Showcase Inc., Puyallup, Wash., Allied Steel, Redmond, Wash., Universal Showcase, Woodbridge, Ont., Northwest Building Technology, Seattle, Ontario Store Fixtures, Toronto (fixturing); Kentucky Wood Floors, Louisville, Ky., Hartco Flooring Co., Dallas, Harris Tarkett, Whitehall, Pa. (hardwood flooring); Kaasco Inc., Mukilteo, Wash., The Mercier Group, Los Angeles, GDM, Paramount, Calif. (furniture); Pionite, Auburn, Maine (laminates); Barbizon, Woburn, Mass., Lightolier, Fall River, Mass. (lighting); DK Display, New York; Goldsmith, Long Island City, N.Y., Patina-V, City of Industry, Calif., Pucci, New York (mannequins); Goebel Fixture Co., Hutchinson, Minn., Columbia Showcase, Sun Valley, Calif., Fetzer's, Salt Lake City, Pacific Coast Showcase, Puyallup, Wash. (millwork); Messenger Sign, Seattle (signage/graphics); Innovative Design Technologies, Valencia, Calif. (special effects for Halogen Department); ArcCom Fabrics, Orangeburg, N.Y., Innovations in Wallcoverings, New York, Carolyn Ray, Yonkers, N.Y., Blumenthal, Canaan, Conn. (wallcoverings)

Photography
Chris Eden, Seattle

Vega

WASHINGTON, D.C.

"Eyebite" is designer Stephen Watkins' term for one form/one ingredient in a space that becomes the central element off which all others play. For Vega, a home design store, the eyebite is a monolithic curved and textured wall, free of hard corners and right angles. Elliptical aluminum shelving provides an innovative way to display the store's collection of accessories, lighting, tableware, linens and other home-furnishing items. A curtain wall of silver woven industrial plastic, projected images of falling water, a rubberized vinyl floor and unexpected touches of bright color complete the multi-textured environment.

Client
Vega International, Washington, D.C. – Jenny Pedersen, owner

Design Team
Stephen Watkins Design Inc., New York – Stephen Watkins, designer; Mitsuyo Nishimura, associate designer; Wade Pranaprom, assistant

Suppliers
Carnegie, Rockville Centre, N.Y. (wall fabric); French Seams, Washington, D.C. (curtains); HMC Inc., Columbia, Md. (desks); Yuka Hosota, New York (textured wall finish); Regency Distributors, New York (lighting); Dry Nature, New York (props and decoratives); Plasticland, New York (Plexiglas® shelves); Brian Jones, Smithfield, Va. (metalwork); Studio Santalla, Washington, D.C. (graphics); Sign Concepts, Springfield, Va. (signage); Arakawa, Portland, Ore. (hanging cable system)

Photography
Timothy Bell, New York

Hot Topic

CITY OF INDUSTRY, CALIF.

The 2200-square-foot prototype offers a "kinetic, industrial-tech feel" within a hip, urban club setting. A 12-foot-long tunnel of faux-rusted steel beams composes the entrance. Changing color-washes create a sense of movement in the tunnel and the store. Industrial insulating material, often used in clubs for sound control, adorns the walls and ceilings of the space. Overscaled metal etagere wall units are backwashed with red lighting; even the cashwrap is underlit with neon lighting.

Client Team:
Hot Topic, City of Industry, Calif. – Orvil Madden, founder; Betsy McLaughlin, president, ceo; Cindy Levitt, vp, general merchandise manager; Karen Talley, vp, accessories; Mark Bertone, vp, real estate, construction; John Gatturna, construction manager

Design Team
JGA Inc., Southfield, Mich. – Kenneth Nisch, chair; Kim Abruscato, senior designer; Arvin Stephenson, project manager; Stephanie Bourdon, creative resource manager

Outside Consultants
June Lester Design, Berkley, Mich. (design collaborator); Douglas Greene, Studio City, Calif. (architect); Deforest Construction, Riverside, Calif. (general contractor); Gary Steffy Lighting Design, Ann Arbor, Mich. (lighting)

Suppliers
K- Metal, Santa Fe Springs, Calif. (cashwrap); Silverface Celotex Insulation Sheathing, Tampa, Fla. (ceiling); Aged Woods, York, Pa., Matworks, Baltimore, Lonseal, Carson, Calif. (flooring); Color Kinetics, Boston, Canlet by Canplas Inc., Denver, Legion, Brooklyn, N.Y., Lightolier, Fall River, Mass. (lighting); Hamrock, Santa Fe Springs, Calif. (metal fixturing); Sherwin-Williams Co., Cleveland, Rustoleum, Vernon Hills, Ill., Benjamin Moore & Co., Montvale, N.J. (paint); Spacewall Intl., Atlanta (slatwall); L.M. Schofield Co., Douglasville, Ga. (stained concrete); Greneker, Los Angeles (storefront theming); C.F. Stinson, Rochester, Mich. (wallcoverings); Armstrong World Industries, Lancaster, Pa. (tile)

Photography
Laszlo Regos Photography, Berkley, Mich.

Bokoo Bikes

CHANHASSEN, MINN.

Bokoo Bikes opened a prototype store in a natural setting next to a bike trail so customers could test-ride the merchandise. Custom-built fixtures incorporate bike parts, such as tires, bolts and hardware. "Curvalicious" bike displays at the front entrance spotlight the "bicycle of the moment." And counters with bar stools encourage customers to lounge while planning bike trips, contemplating purchases or waiting for bike repairs.

Client
Vigil Companies Ltd., Eden Prairie, Minn. – Ed Vigil, owner

Design Team
Interior Systems Inc., Fond du Lac, Wis. – Shannon Hakala, designer; Kari Muenster, creative director; Stacey Olin, sales

Architect
Lampert Architects, Ham Lake, Minn. – Len Hampert, senior project designer; Ed Romo, head designer/initial conception

General Contractor
Amcon Construction, Burnsville, Minn.

Suppliers
Sony, Tokyo (audio/video); Duralee Fabrics, Bay Shore, N.Y. (fabrics); 3M Colorquartz, St. Paul, Minn., Blue Ridge Carpet, Ellijay, Ga. (flooring); Interior Systems Inc., Fond du Lac, Wis. (fixturing, graphics); Halo Lighting, Peachtree City, Ga. (lighting); Nevamar, Odenton, Md., Laminart, Elk Grove Village, Ill., Arborite, LaSalle Que. (laminates); Sign Images, Osseo, Minn. (signage); Innovations in Wallcoverings, New York (wallcoverings)

Photography
Steve Hanke, Minneapolis

Marshall Field's

CHICAGO

To suit Armani's fragrance, "Mania," Marshall Field's designed illuminated echtechromes in nickel frames for the brand's advertising. Fourteen-foot black fabric covered archways in the entrances to the fragrance department, while low music intended to represent the human pulse played in the background. The focal point of the presentation was a four-sided cube suspended 20 feet above the floor, which featured engraved line patterns, logos and ebbing light.

Client Design Team
L'Oreal USA Inc., New York – Doug Huffmyer, assistant vp creative director, designer fragrances

Design Team
Marshall Field's, Chicago/The Department Store Division of Target Corp., Minneapolis – Jamie Becker, creative director of visual marketing; Jon Jones, visual specialist, cosmetics; Jennifer Moryc, merchandise presentation manager; Donna Milano Johnson, windows; Amy Meadows, visual marketing manager; Molly Begala, visual merchandising

Outside Design Consultants
Pepper Construction, Chicago

Suppliers
Frost Lighting, Chicago (lighting); 555 Automatic, Chicago, Color Image, Chicago, Look, New York (props); Goldleaf Plastics, Waite Park, Minn. (plastics)

Photography
Susan Kezon, Chicago

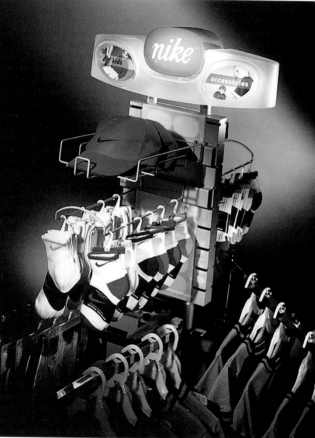

Uf Playwear

GREENSBORO, N.C.

Powdercoated sheet metal and tubing, combined with a black polyethylene back panel, composed this Nike fixture display for VF Playwear. Designed by the Beeline Group to help shoppers spot the Nike kids' products, the lit acrylic header bears the brand name in simple, toy-like script and shapes.

Client Team
VF Playwear, Greensboro, N.C. – Joanna Beddingfield, marketing manager

Design Team
Beeline Group Inc., Newark, Calif. – Kevin Sullivan, senior account executive; Brian Milano, designer; Greg Raub, project manager

Photography
Kevin Ng Photography, San Francisco, Calif.

Carolee

GREENWICH, CONN.

This 600-square-foot boutique is dedicated to selling a total lifestyle, not just the retailer's signature lines of jewelry, handbags and home accessories. The intimate setting relies on a palette ranging from sea-green glass to natural wood fixtures and white walls and flooring to create a sense of space and elegance. Custom showcases allow customers to open and close drawers while examining merchandise.

Design Team
Vignelli Associates, New York (interior design, graphic design) – Massimo Vignelli, Lella Vignelli, Sharon Singer, Yoshimi Kono, Yuji Yamazaki, design team

Lighting Design
Fisher Marantz Stone, New York

General Contractor
Richter+Ratner Contracting Corp., Maspeth, N.Y. (general contractor, millwork, fixtures)

Suppliers
Lightolier, Fall River, Mass., Bartco, Huntington Beach, Calif., Specialty Lighting, Shelby, N.C. (lighting); Benjamin Moore Paint Co., Montvale, N.J. (paint)

Photography
Elliot Kaufman, Elliot Kaufman Photography, New York

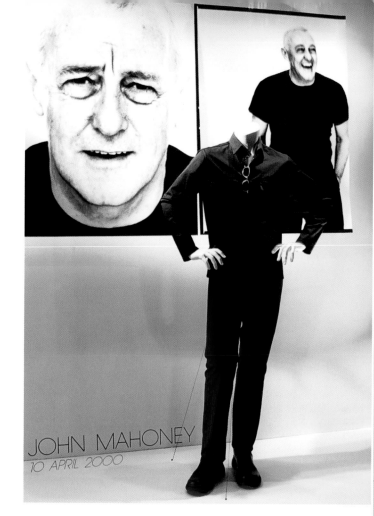

JOHN MAHONEY
10 APRIL 2000

STEPPENWOLF

25

SKREBNESKI

MARTHA PLIMPTON

SKREB

My friend Victor is an actor: didn't you know? But he doesn't have a theater, he has a studio. And he uses unusual exotic stage-craft. Things like light, color, shade, mystery, line, elegance, composition, drama, personality, bravura, sensuality, emotion, humor, precision, mood, control and passion. All scripted with a large measure of love for the sheer beauty of his subjects. Yes, in one play! Most wonderful actors and artists are magicians. It takes art and magic and actor's special charisma, to make "a Skrebneski". They're unforgettable and instantly recognized. And if greatness lies in originality and uniqueness, well, his work is a masterpiece of both. Making art is hard work, but Victor likes the drama, so he's always on stage. Though my friend Victor doesn't actually act he's a Tony-award winner!

Marshall Field's

CHICAGO

To commemorate Steppenwolf Theatre's 25th anniversary, photographer Victor Skrebneski created the book, "Steppenwolf 25: A Photographic Celebration of an Actor's Theatre." Marshall Field's State Street store blew up select photos from the book to 6-foot-by-12-foot images, backed by white walls and floors for a gallery-feel. White, headless mannequins in black fashions contributed to the personalities of the portraits. The red Steppenwolf logo, silk-screened on the glass, offered a touch of color.

Client Design Team
Marshall Field's State Street, Chicago/The Department Store Division of Target Corp., Minneapolis – Donna Milano Johnson, window display specialist; Amy Meadows, visual marketing manager; Jamie Becker, creative director of visual marketing

Outside Design Consultant
Victor Skrebneski, Chicago

Suppliers
Color Image, Chicago (graphics)

Photography
Susan Kezon, Chicago

STEPPENWOLF

In the past twenty-five years, the legendary Steppenwolf Theatre Company of Chicago has redefined the landscape of acting and performance in America, spawning a generation of actors and directors. No other American acting ensemble has survived as long and thrived as much as the steppenwolf ensemble of artists. The company is: Joan Allen, Kevin Anderson, Randall Arney, Robert Breuler, Gary Cole, Kathryn Erbe, K. Todd Freeman, Frank Galati, Francis Guinan, Moira Harris, Glenne Headly, Tim Hopper, Tom Irwin, Terry Kinney, Tina Landau, Martha Lavey, John Mahoney, John Malkovich, Mariann Mayberry, Laurie Metcalf, Amy Morton, Sally Murphy, Austin Pendleton, Jeff Perry, Martha Plimpton, Rondi Reed, Molly Regan, Eric Simonson, Gary Sinise, Lois Smith, Rick Snyder, Jim True-Frost and Alan Wilder.

STEPPENWOLF
25
SKREBNESKI

FRANK GALATI

STEPPENWOLF
25
SKREBNESKI

fresh

NEW YORK

A store in New York's NoLita neighborhood marks the bath and beauty retailer's third location. Light is supplied by 1960s-era fixtures, while white predominates the color palette. The fixtures are on legs to create an open feeling. A gradated color tile pattern travels the length of the space, from dark to light to dark again.

Client Team
Fresh Inc., Boston – Lev Glazman, Alina Roytberg, owners

Design Team
Hacin & Associates Inc., Boston – David Hacin, president; Aaron Weinert, project manager

Outside Design Consultant
Fountainhead, Marshfield, Mass. (solid surfacing)

Suppliers
Harvey Electronics, New York (audio/visual); Comatec Inc., Woodbridge, Ont. (fixturing and furniture); American Olean, Dallas (tile flooring); Danalite, Cerritos, Calif., Juno Lighting, DesPlaines, Ill. (lighting); Spectrum Sign, New York (signage)

Photography
Chuck Choi Architectural Photography, Brooklyn, N.Y.

| displays/fixtures |

Stride Rite

NATICK, MASS.

This 825-square-foot kids' shoe store prototype features chunky, playful fixtures and a soft color palette, creating a fun yet residential feel. Fixtures stand no higher than two feet and resemble furnishings that appeal to children, like bureaus and bookshelves with colorful, spinning handles. Bleached oak and maple surfaces brighten the space.

Client Design
Stride Rite Corp., Lexington, Mass. – Jerry Silverman, president, Stride Rite children's group; Donna Morton, senior vp, brand creative; Jan Nannicelli, senior vp, operations; Barbara Scott, senior vp, retail merchandising; Midge Kirby, director, visual merchandising; James Harte, manager, design and construction

Design Team
Chute Gerdeman Inc., Columbus, Ohio – Lee Peterson, executive vp, brand strategies; Eric Eberhardt, program manager, environments; Scot Townley, senior designer, environments; Jennifer Linn, brand strategies; Maribeth Gatchalian, designer, environments; Jennifer Bajec, senior designer, graphics; Mary Jane Picard, designer, graphics; Heidi Brandewie, senior visual merchandising; Nicole Vachow, visual merchandising; Carmen Costinescu, materials resourcing; Kendall Cobb, implementation; Lori Frame, production manager; Susan Siewny, graphic production

Suppliers
B&N Industries, San Carlos, Calif., Custom Surroundings, Valley City, Ohio (fixturing); Atlas Carpet Mills, Los Angeles, Masland Carpet, Saraland, Ala. (flooring); Brentano, Northbrook, Ill. (fabric); Trout Studios, Culver City, Calif. (footstools); Excell Business Systems, Columbus, Ohio (furniture); Skeeles Mfg., Columbus, Ohio, Image West, Grand Rapids, Mich. (visual merchandising elements); Duron Paint & Wallcoverings, Beltsville, Md. (wallcovering); Armstrong World Industries, Lancaster, Pa. (ceiling elements); Digico Imaging, Columbus, Ohio, Image West, Grand Rapids, Mich., KSK Color Lab, Cleveland (signage); Atlite, White Plains, N.Y., Flos USA Inc., Huntington Station, N.Y., Hera Lighting Systems, Atlanta, Tango Lighting, N. Bergen, N.J., Zaneen, Toronto (lighting); Lighting Management, New City, N.Y. (lighting coordination); Treehouse Development Corp., Lake Mary, Fla. (contractor)

Photography
Mark Steele Photography, Columbus, Ohio

Creative Kidstuff

PITTSBURGH

Catering to shoppers at Pittsburgh Intl. Airport looking for treasures to bring home to their kids, the 1400-square-foot store is an oasis of colors, shapes and pictures. Colorful, undulating patterns and whimsical architectural elements lead shoppers through the space. Wheeled floor fixtures and brightly painted nesting tables provide flexible merchandising for the store's unique toy offering.

Client Team
    CBR Inc., St. Paul, Minn. – Carole Howe, president; Cynthia Gerdes, president, Creative Kidstuff; Abby Rutchick, vp of merchandsing, Creative Kidstuff

Design Team
    James Henke Design, Minneapolis – James Henke, principal; Lami Grub Architects, Pittsburgh – Susan Lami, principal; CBR Inc., St. Paul, Minn. – Carole Howe, president

Suppliers
    Madsen Fixture & Millwork, Forest Lake, Minn. (fixtures); Sign Innovation, Harmony, Pa. (storefront sign); Metro Floor, Greenwich, Conn. (flooring)

Photography
    David Neiman, Edina, Minn.

Index of Designers

Index of Merchants